THE TRINITY

Balancing Body, Mind and Soul

Megha Baweja

ISBN
Paperback 979-8-89777-245-2
Hardcase 979-8-89777-246-9

Made with ♥ on the Notion Press Platform

www.notionpress.com

Dedication

To my beloved family,
For your unwavering support, endless sacrifices,
and boundless love. You have gone the extra mile to provide
me with the gift of knowledge and the foundation to chase my
dreams. This book is a reflection of the values you've instilled
in me—the pursuit of balance, wisdom, and purpose.

I am forever grateful.

Contents

Preface

In the downfall of my life, when the weight of struggles seemed unbearable, books became my best friends. They offered solace, wisdom, and a path forward when I felt lost. Each page I turned became a stepping stone toward self-improvement, teaching me that growth is not a destination but a journey—one that requires balance in all aspects of life.

I began searching for a way to align my body, mind, and soul. I read countless philosophies, explored different spiritual teachings, and experimented with various practices. What I discovered was profound: true transformation happens when these three elements exist in harmony. Without a strong body, the mind struggles. Without a clear mind, the soul is restless. And without a nourished soul, life feels empty, no matter how much we achieve.

This book is for all those who seek to improve their lives by finding that balance. It is not just about physical health, mental strength, or spiritual enlightenment alone, but about how these three aspects intertwine to create a fulfilling life.

If you've ever felt stuck, overwhelmed, or disconnected from yourself, know that you are not alone. This book is a guide—a companion on your journey to aligning your body, mind, and soul so that you can live with purpose, clarity, and peace.

I invite you to embark on this journey with me, to explore, reflect, and apply these lessons in your own life. May you find the balance you seek and, in doing so, unlock the limitless potential within you.

Megha

09.03.2025

Acknowledgments

Writing this book has been a journey of growth, learning, and self-discovery, and I could not have done it alone.

First and foremost, my deepest gratitude goes to my family. Your unwavering love, encouragement, and belief in my dreams have been the foundation of my strength. Thank you for always pushing me to reach higher and for the sacrifices you have made to provide me with the best opportunities in life. This book is as much yours as it is mine.

To my friends, who have stood by me through every challenge and triumph—your support, patience, and words of motivation have meant the world to me. You have cheered me on, reminded me of my purpose, and kept me grounded through this creative journey.

Lastly, to all the authors whose words have inspired me—thank you for igniting the spark within me to write. Your stories, wisdom, and dedication to the craft have been my guiding light. This book is a testament to the impact that great writing can have on a person's soul. With immense gratitude,

Megha

Introduction

In the fast-paced world we live in, finding balance between the body, mind, and soul can feel like an impossible task. We are constantly pulled in different directions—work, relationships, responsibilities—often neglecting the very core of our well-being. But true fulfillment doesn't come from just achieving success or acquiring knowledge; it comes from aligning these three essential aspects of our being.

The Trinity: Balancing Body, Mind, and Soul is a guide to achieving this harmony. This book is for anyone seeking a deeper connection with themselves, a healthier lifestyle, and a clearer sense of purpose. It explores how our physical health, mental clarity, and spiritual awareness are interconnected and how, when nurtured together, they can lead to a more enriched and meaningful life.

Through a blend of personal experiences, research, and practical insights, this book provides a roadmap to help you strengthen your body, calm your mind, and nourish your soul. Whether you are starting your journey or looking to refine your path, the principles within these pages will empower you to live with greater balance and inner peace.

My hope is that, as you read through this book, you find inspiration, guidance, and the motivation to embrace a lifestyle that fosters true well-being. The journey begins now—one step at a time toward a healthier, happier, and more harmonious you.

Megha

Part 1

THE TRINITY WITHIN US

Chapter 1
The Power of Balance

" Happiness is not a matter of intensity but of balance, order, rhythm, and harmony."

– Thomas Merton

Let's start with a simple truth: It is said that life is not a game of checkers; it's more like trying to perform in a circus and failing horribly at it, like juggling with chainsaws while riding a unicycle on a rope. Sounds dramatic? Maybe. But that is how most people feel when they attempt to straighten out the physical, mental, and spiritual aspects of their lives. If only one thing starts to turn in the wrong direction, then suddenly everything gives that falling off-a-cliff impression.

To understand balance, let's take an example of a three-legged stool. Each leg represents one aspect of your being: body, mind, and soul. All three legs must be strong; then you can sit both solid and sure. But what if one of them, or more, is too short? Too long? Entirely absent? Prepare yourself for quite an ungainly fall. (Okay, and do you know what? You cannot just screw the pieces together with duct tape – it just won't do.).

Now, just suppose you want to balance on that uncomfortable stool, and the floor below starts bobbing in various directions. One moment, it can be stable as a rock, and the next, you almost feel like you're wobbling off the edge. Life never ceases to challenge your stability, and no matter how hard you try to strengthen your bowl, something is always going to rock the boat. It is not simply enough to ensure that each leg is the correct length; however, adaptability and fine tuning is required to always keep the structure in balance. Life isn't standing still with a list of dos and don'ts, it goes on to the extent of demanding that you be more specific, come up with better defense mechanisms no matter the fact that you feel like you are about to fall.

Let's start with a story—a real-life tale of imbalance that we've all been part of:

The "Body Only" Guy

Meet Rahul. Rahul's life motto is: "Lift, bro!" He's the fellow who spends days at the gym; drinks protein shakes as if it were some divine juices and contemplates his mirror-like any surface that shines. But here's the thing: Though he might be able to pick up a watermelon with his hands, Rahul does not know when he last read a book, performed any kind of meditation, or had a healthy conversation not related to his new record at bench pressing. Result? Rahul is living proof that gods must have white skin, chiseled features, and a great build because he could otherwise be a true example of emotional and mental chaos.

Moral of the story? Too much attention to the outside and complete dismissal of the interior makes you into a beautiful work of art but devoid of consciousness.

The "Mind-Overload" Friend

Now, meet Neha. Neha is completely the opposite of Rahul. She lives in her head 24/7. Her concept of what constitutes "fitness" is hauling piles of self-actualization tomes picked up at the local bookstore back to the office. In addition, she knows how to do everything much better than millions of people, remembers all the numerous applications for improving productivity, and can recite all the philosophers, from Socrates to Alan Watts. But here's the catch: Neha's body is always weary (she has sleep four hours a night), and the last thing she did for her spirit was that she attempted yoga and failed half ways through the Sun Salutation.

Result? Neha's mind is a Ferrari, but her body and soul are two bicycles that have their tires deflated. Not much going on here in terms of progress

The "Spiritual Only" Uncle

Last but not the least, let's have some discussion on Uncle Raj. Uncle Raj has moved to a higher realm – this is how it has been put. Or so he claims. He sits around practicing yoga, reciting the sacred Vedas, and informing everyone they are falling into the 'rat race' of the West. But here's the twist: Uncle Raj hasn't even twitched in decades (except for the fingers that swipe his phone to ensure he receives enough 'spiritual healer' likes) and is delusional to the extent of believing Bitcoin is some form of mindfulness.

His imbalance? To me, speaking of the soul as a thing apart from a healthy body or a curious mind gives spirituality a... slightly crazy air.

Why Balance Matters

With Rahul, Neha, and Uncle Raj, you have learned why the world needs balance. Being lonely, each of them lacks something essential in his or her life and feels the emptiness. Now, let us understand that the differences between the body, mind, and soul are not contrary to three different superheroes, but they are the Avengers team. And as with any team, you being a patient, they must cooperate to save you.

Here's the secret: when the body is healthy, it engages the mind. I always like to think that clarity in the mind is food for the soul. And that when the soul is satisfied, it animates the body. That's the cycle, not a competition.

The Humor in Imbalance

Let's face it: Because life will always have its share of uneven and off-kilter moments, they really give ha-ha moments. Just as in one episode, you said, 'Hey, it's time to focus on my soul; I'm headed for a silent retreat' and found out you cannot make it five without posting a picture on Instagram. Or when you told yourself that you would be jogging in the morning by 6 a.m., while in actual sense you were servicing a pizza dough with the 'arm curl.'

The problem here is that you shouldn't take yourself all that seriously. Sure, balance isn't perfect— it is learning how to walk and maybe even how to dance the tango and fall gracefully or even laugh.

A Final Thought

In the end, nurturing body, mind, spirit doesn't mean turning into some sort of New Age hippie who ate kale, spends hours in lotus position and drop Nietzsche quotes at every turn. It is exactly the encouragement of getting up a little each day and giving yourself love in all three aspects of your being. You might take a brief walk in the park (body), turn to an interesting article (mind), and spend 5 min watching the sunset (spirit).

Remember: In fact, the work of balance is less action-oriented and more state-oriented. And if you, from time to time, topple off that figurative stool? Laughs, just dust yourself and retry again. But hey, even the most skilled juggler will always find ways and lose some of the balls sometimes.

In fact, true balance means striking the best balance as often as possible, and being kind to oneself when balanced isn't quite possible. Sometimes, you might concentrate fully on just one aspect of the body, and for the remaining parts, you would forget all about them. On other days, your mind will be racing with so many thoughts that your soul may not even get a glimpse. That's okay. The goal shouldn't be to keep things as perfect and balanced as possible but to make small corrections when you lose that alignment. And by the time you are done with it, you shall discover that, seeking balance IS self-love. Like any other relationship, the one you have with yourself also needs time, energy, and consistency, and most importantly, do not forget that life begins in the moment.

Chapter 2
The Body as the Foundation

<blockquote>

The body is your temple. Keep it pure and clean for the soul to reside in."

– B.K.S. Iyengar

</blockquote>

Let's get one thing straight: your body is not just an elegant garment in which you travel – it is the primary form of your existence. It's as important as the Wi-Fi router in your house. If not, Netflix (mind) is not working, soul is stuck in a never ending 'buffering' while your Spotify meditation playlist plays in the background. All in all, as the body gives way, so does the rest of it.

But let's be real: cynicism is that most of us use our body as a rental car. We work all the life out of them, fail to feed them right and only care when the check engine light comes on. Sound familiar? Well, it is about time that changed, and this is why.

The Pizza-Over-Salad Dilemma

First off, there is nutrition—because if the body is the operating system, then, what you choose to input is your nutrient. In our minds let's picture that you are high performance status symbol of a sports car (and indeed some days you felt more akin to the second-hand scooter). Would you put the best fuel into it, or add used soda and fries? As it goes with most of us, unfortunately, we opt for the fries.

For instance, my friend Ravi can easily be considered. Ravi loves junk food. A burger, a chip, a fried samosa—you think that Ravi has not gulped these down umpteen times. But with the one too many 'post-lunch crashes and the fateful morning, he dozed off in the middle of the meeting and snored louder than I'd ever admit; Ravi decided it was high time he listened to his body. Well, he altered things – actually, did not turn things around dramatically; he just changed. He decided to consume more fruits, replaced soda with water, and discovered an alchemist's secret of the vegetable smoothie. But within weeks, Ravi seemed to have the energy of an eleven-year-old again. His mind was somehow in a better state, and what do you know? He even signed up for a 5K run (and lived).

The lesson? Food is not only about the size anymore. This energizes the brain, makes you happy, and gives your spirit the power to glow.

Fitness: More Than Just Gym Selfies

Now let us discuss exercise we've heard so much about it but really what does it mean from a physiological point of view? So, you don't have to go to gym and grunt like a bodybuilder or become that crazy CrossFit fanatic who flips tires in their spare time.\. Basically, fitness is as simple as the act of exercising and I will assure you, it is life changing.

Consider, for instance, Pooja – my irremovable source of stressed colleague. Her shoulders were somewhere around her ears, and any effort she considered as moving was just picking up her phone to scroll through snippets of other people's lives on Instagram. Yet, one fine morning, she thought of doing Yoga. It started as a joke: she could not even bend her legs to touch the ground without groaning, but within a month, it became a routine for her to do the Sun Salutations. The best part? Pooja's stress melted away. She started sleeping better, her thinking became less foggy, and she did not get snappy during meetings. Turns out, moving your body doesn't just improve your health—it changes your entire vibe.

And if Yoga isn't your thing? Walk, dance, swim, cycle, or just take stairs instead of elevators. Movement is a medicine; it doesn't mean it has to be fancy; it only needs to be consistent.

Rest: The Most Underrated Superpower

Let's not forget the one thing everyone loves, but no one gets enough of: **sleep**. Your body isn't a machine that requires constant work; it needs downtime to rest and restore. But how often do we sacrifice sleep for late-night Netflix binges, work deadlines, or scrolling through TikTok until our eyeballs protest?

I once met a guy who bragged about only sleeping four hours a night. "Sleep is for the weak!" he'd say. Fast forward six months, and he was falling asleep at his desk, his creativity tanked, and he got so cranky that people started avoiding him altogether. Spoiler alert: he finally listened to his doctor and prioritized sleep—and surprisingly, he became productive, happy, and (most importantly) tolerable to be around again.

Moral of the story? Sleep isn't laziness. It's the best possible life hack for your body, mind, and soul.

The Body-Mind-Soul Triangle

Well, that's where the fun lies. If the body is fed, moved, and rested, the mind and soul follow along. Have you ever observed that a good exercise helps your mind to get focused; similarly, whenever you eat a healthy meal, you feel… lighter somehow? That's no coincidence.

Healthy body does not only carry, but also energizes, lifts emotions and prepares heart to find anew of its kind of experiences. When you switch from a slow, badly performing computer to a state of the art one that performs exceptionally well, it is like this. Suddenly everything gets done with ease.

The Humor in Neglect

Of course, everyone remembers the moments when we completely ignore our bodies and, in the future, the situation looks funny. To say the least, you believed that it was a good idea to consume three slices of cake at once – and then you crashed. Or when you attempted a workout video, failed at following the instructor, and wind up too tired to even sit, just lying on the floor with deep thoughts. (Been there, done that.)

Not worrying is a good lesson to learn; the more you focus on it, the more you mess up. Instead, laugh it off and start fresh. In other words, the body is remarkably forgiving as long as you're willing to meet it halfway.

A Final Thought

When it comes to the way you treat your body, think of it as the structure of a house. If it's weak, the entire edifice—that is, your mind (the walls) and your soul (the roof) begin to crumble. But when you've built a good structure that's sound, you are ready to take on any situation.

But here's the catch: And let's face it, balance is not about getting it right in the middle, but it's about getting it right repeatedly. Every day will be different; there will be moments and days where all your thoughts are spinning, your body is exhausted, and your spirit is lost. That's okay. The art of life is not about getting to a desert of equilibrium but about regaining one's balance when the world has knocked one off course.

The fact is that real life will never let it snowball; it will always continue giving you curve balls to try to catch. End-of-the-week pressure, an unplanned obstacle, or that slice of cake that sneaked into the diet – all are manageable. The question is not what has been done to you. However, if you consider balance as a process rather than getting to that state, you can look at any fall and learn more about how to be stable faster, smarter, and firmer in your position.

Thus, consume the salad (though even embrace the pizza sometimes). Get up and exercise (it doesn't have to be much; even going for a walk is fine). Oh yeah and use one of the best gifts you've been given in life, and sleep. I will still recall that moderation it is not a confined cycle of no enjoyment, but it is a cycle where enjoyment, regulation, and rest are made to fit.

And here's the beautiful part: this is when, your body is healthy, your mind is clear, and the soul starts to glow. It is a cycle: a perpetual and nurturing cycle whereby every aspect of your being is an encouragement to the other.

In the end, seeking balance is not about perfection; it's about kindness—kindness toward your body, patience with your mind, and compassion for your soul. Because, just like a tree that bends with the wind yet stands firm, true balance is about flexibility, resilience, and the simple joy of living fully in the moment.

Chapter 3
The Mind as the Navigator

> **❝ The mind is everything.
> What you think you become."**
>
> *– Buddha*

Imagine yourself as if you are the captain of a ship in the middle of the ocean with turbulent waters most of the time. Your body is the vehicle, your soul the destination, and the mind, well, it's the engine, the navigator. The mind navigates, maps the star trek, and determines whether your flight will be smooth sailing or end up like the Titanic, sinking into an iceberg with the ship's company (minus the dramatic music and floating door).

The mind is strong I have no doubt about it. But here's the catch: It is also kind of like an over-caffeine squirrel. If not kept in check, it will jump from one thought to the next, one worry to the next, one idea to the next before you can say, 'Calm down! Mental clarity, emotional intelligence, and mindfulness aren't just optional—they're the tools you need to keep your inner squirrel from running the show.

Mental Clarity: The Brain's Decluttering Service

Consider coming into a room crowded with clutter, clothes scattered on the floor, dirty dishes in the sink, and papers scattered all around. That's what it is like to have an unorganized mind. You are attempting to concentrate, but your mind is as messy as that room, and suddenly, choosing what to eat for lunch looks like a Rubik's Cube decision.

Now, meet my friend Meera. Meera was the queen of having a cluttered mind. This woman would wake up with work deadlines preoccupying her mind, her mom's doctor appointment, a conversation she had with her boss last week that she wished she handled differently, and the issue of global warming. Her brain was fried by 10 a.m. One day, one of her friends advised her to perform the 'mental cleaning' with the help of constructing a list of thoughts and choosing the three most vital ones. The result? But for Meera, it wasn't just about getting more accomplished — she felt unbearably relieved after dusting up all the clutter in her head.

Mental clarity is like Marie Kondo for your brain: it makes you eliminate distractions so that you can concentrate on things that bring joy (or the next best thing). Things as basic as writing what you want to or can do in a day, dividing large tasks into subtasks, etc., can work havoc.

Emotional Intelligence: The Art of Not Losing Your Cool

Let's be honest: I believe that we are all aware of those moments in our lives when we want nothing more than to flip a table. Whether it is the colleague who continuously fails to include you in copies of emails, that hooligan who violates the lanes in traffic, even to the cousin/ aunt/ uncle, whoever asks you about when you are planning to get married again having done it about a hundred times. Life tests your patience daily.

Of course, that's where emotional intelligence comes in. It is the ultimate power that assist individuals to take a deep breath and be well mannered in their response instead of letting your inner Hulk smash everything in sight.

Take my neighbor, Ramesh. It was well known that Ramesh had a short fuse. He chronicles his life and problems, and one day, one customer service agent put him on hold, and he yelled at the person on the phone for that, so he decided to work on his emotional intelligence. He started practicing something called "the 3-second rule": whenever he felt angry, he would take some time normally the count to three and then react. In the beginning, it was rather strange, though later, it became rather effective. Ramesh stopped being "that guy," and even his wife started calling him "Zen Ramesh."

Emotional intelligence is not the absence of anger, or the ability to control angry feelings—it's a person's capacity to have effective emotional experiences, recognizing the emotions of others, and successfully manage the self–other interface in ways that foster positive outcomes.

Mindfulness: Training the Squirrel

Alright now let's get down to the elephant on the table, mindfulness or the mother of all the hacks to curb the run-away brain. Mindfulness is the act of being present – present. It's about appreciating the wind against your skin or the taste of your coffee or the chirping of birds rather than focusing on the existing horrifying news.

Take Priya, for instance. Priya was one of the most 'busy bees' that anyone could ever come across. She'd eat lunch with her eyes focused on the computer, arrange meetings while taking her dog for a walk, and mentally rehearse the entire workday before she gets to sleep. But one day, she tried a mindfulness exercise: appreciatively savoring a chocolate bar to the last crumb by paying as much attention to it as humanly possible. It blew her mind. For the first time, Priya realized how much she'd been rushing through life without really living it.

Mindfulness isn't about meditation alone (though that helps). It's about enjoying and living in the present, and that can be done while eating, walking, and doing dishes. It's about purposefully paying attention to things around you instead of letting it blur past you.

The Mind-Body-Soul Connection

Here's the thing: a clear, emotionally intelligent, and mindful mind doesn't just help itself—it uplifts the body and soul too. When your mind is cleared, your body doesn't feel as tight. Emotional intelligence means even if things are tough, your relationships are growing, and that's good for your soul. And when you're mindful, you do appreciate something as simple as that and as a result nourishing all three components of your being.

It's like driving a car: The physical body is a car, the soul is the gasoline, and the mind is the wheel. If the mind is not in control, you're either stuck in the park or in a ditch at the side of the road.

The Humor in Overthinking

Of course, the mind isn't always easy to manage. Sometimes, it spirals into overthinking mode, and you find yourself awake at 3 a.m., wondering if you accidentally offended someone 12 years ago. Or you spend 20 minutes analyzing whether the "ok" someone texted you mean "ok" or "not ok." (Spoiler: It probably just means "ok.")

The good news? The power of your mind remains impressive, yet its erratic nature should be viewed as a source of humorous reminders. It's like an over dramatic friend who makes everything become melodramatic despite being unreliable.

A Final Thought

The mind controls the direction that a person's life takes, but being the captain of a ship, it must have the tools and knowledge. That is why achieving clarity of mind, sensitivity, and spiritual maturity allows to set up a clear course, avoid wasting time on drama and really enjoy the process.

Think of it this way: The trip that is called life is not a race to the finish line but a beautiful journey, with each act to be savored along the way. Suppose that your thoughts shape the painting of your life: then every thought is a stroke, and every moment – is an attempt to take a beautiful picture. And just like any artist, your mind thrives when it's nurtured, guided, and given the space to focus on what truly matters.

Therefore, clear your mind, count to ten before responding, and enjoy the little things, whether sitting in bumper-to-bumper traffic or having to describe, 'I have no idea where I will be in five years' for the tenth time. Life's better when your inner navigator is calm, focused, and just a little bit amused.

Chapter 4
The Soul as the Essence

> **The soul is placed in the body like a rough diamond, and it must be polished, or the luster of it will never appear."**
>
> *– Daniel Defoe*

While the body engulfs you and the mind guides you, the soul is the reason or the desire that drives the whole process. So, to give it the analogy, most would understand it is the icing on the cake, or the cherry on top, or the secret ingredient that really ties the meal together. Yes, the body and mind can go through life without it, yet something feels off, or more accurately, nearly bland. It's the part of you that wishes there was more to life than work, bills, grocery shopping, and struggling to recall your Netflix password.

Let's face it: However, to set such a pace, we spend so much time focusing on the outside: our bodies, our careers, our wallets, and overlooking the inside. And that's where the soul comes into play, whispering to us, "Hey, what about me?" (Except the soul doesn't nag—it's way too classy for that.)

Spirituality: It's Not Just About Chanting or Incense

First things first: Spirituality is not the mere practice of yoga with closed eyes, chanting Om while somebody burns sandalwood incense next to you. It's not about taking a week off work and going to a meditation retreat in the Himalayas (but if that is the choice you love, great). Spirituality is only defined as being in touch with the aspect of you that is aware that the universe is greater than your consciousness.

Take my friend Akash, for example. Akash had never been seen as a religious man, and he also thought of spirituality as something only monks cared about. However, during the worst times of his life, he began volunteering at a shelter. It wasn't planned—his friend dragged him along—but something about helping others made him feel lighter, more alive. Akash realized that spirituality doesn't have to be about rituals; it's about finding what makes your soul feel expansive, whether that's helping people, spending time in nature, or just sitting in silence for a few minutes each day.

It must be added here that spirituality is not a one-stop solution plan that may fit all. It's deeply personal, like your favorite playlist. It's all about identifying what matters to our inner self and creating room for it.

Purpose: Why You Do What You Do

Now, let's talk about purpose. Life specifically relates to your soul when there is something for which to get out of bed in the morning, other than coffee, of course. That is why I speak and write – purpose adds depth to life, like good plot to the movie where people do not blow up in five minutes.

But here's the thing: having meaning in life doesn't mean that there's a mission to save the world or write the next great novel. It can be as mundane as raising a kind child, creating a lovely garden, or even just making people smile.

Take my aunt Sunita. She was married for years and had a high-paying corporate job, but the nature of work was very demanding, stressing her emotionally. He had fun every day after she retired when she began baking cakes for no reason. She successfully started baking cakes at her home, and everyone in her locality wanted to have a bite of her cakes. Therefore, she began a small bakery. Now, she is washing her hands in flour every day, and she is the happiest as she was ever. Her goal was not to save the world; it was to make people happy (as well as cook a few amazing croissants).

It's correct that purpose doesn't have to be grand; it only needs to be yours. And when you live it, your soul glows like nothing that you could achieve through editing your photo on Instagram.

Connection: The Soul's Favorite Language

The soul craves connection – with other people, with nature, beyond the self and the world, and, of course, within the self. It's like a Wi-Fi signal for your inner being: This is probably why when we are plugged in, everything just seems so right. If, for whatever reason, you're disconnected, you feel like you are floating in the vastness of the middle of nowhere.

Let me give you an example – Ravi (yes, the same Ravi that I have already introduced to you – it seems like there is more to this man than meets the eye). Ravi was more of an introvert who would mostly sit at home, scrolling through social media and watching TV. But then, one day, he joined a community gardening group. It appeared ludicrous, but there was a method in the madness: the camaraderie of working with his hands, chatting with the neighbors, and seeing plants grow brought him a kind of joy he hadn't felt in years. Ravi didn't just grow tomatoes—he grew a sense of belonging.

Connection doesn't always come in obvious forms. Sometimes, it's a long conversation with a friend. Sometimes it's staring at a starry sky and realizing how small you are in the grand scheme of things. And sometimes, it's just sitting quietly and listening to your own thoughts without judgment.

The Soul's Subtle Whispers

Now, let's address the elephant in the room: I must admit that the soul doesn't exactly stand up and shout; does it want to be heard? It whispers. It nudges. It is that passive gut sensation that something is correct—or incorrect. The problem? Most of us are busy with our work and running from one chore to another that we cannot hear it.

I once read about a woman who said her soul spoke to her during a particularly mundane activity: washing the dishes. As she stood there, hands in soapy water, she suddenly felt an overwhelming sense of peace and gratitude. It was a small, fleeting moment, but it reminded her to slow down and appreciate life's simplest pleasures.

The soul doesn't need grand gestures. It doesn't demand candlelit rituals or mountaintop retreats (though it wouldn't say no to those). It just needs you to pause, breathe, and pay attention.

The Humor in "Finding Yourself"

Let's be honest: It can often feel as if the more a person's soul searches, the more like an embarrassing game of hide and seek it becomes. This may start as a journaling exercise, and you'll end up drawing cartoon characters. You'll sit comfortably, put in half an hour for meditation, and the other half will be wondering if you left the stove on. Somewhat related, you'll join a yoga class and shortly discover that a bend like that cannot be put into practice.

And that's okay. The soul doesn't need perfection. It knows you're human (and likely a wiggly mess when trying to learn). The point is simply to continue, to never stop in search of what you want and need, and, most importantly, to keep laughing at yourself along the way.

A Final Thought

The soul is the essence of who you are. It's not about how big your house is, how well you've done at work, or how many friends you have on Facebook. It's about basics like that voice deep down inside of you that desires and looks for meaning, relationships, and more than just the job that you do.

But nurturing the soul isn't always about profound revelations; sometimes, it's about the little, ordinary acts that add extraordinary meaning. It is the amused ripple when eating with friends, the tranquility of taking a stroll alone in the woods, or the quiet joy of creating something purely for the love of it. The soul thrives in simplicity, in the moments when you allow yourself to just be.

So, listen to the whispers. Pursue things that give you the chills. And remember: The soul, in other words, is not something that is discovered but developed, day by day, decision by decision.

Because when the soul is nourished, life doesn't just feel meaningful—it feels downright magical

✓ Daily Trinity Checklist

Mind

- Meditate: Morning and night
- Get enough sleep
- Take a mental health walk each morning
- Practice daily affirmations: Morning and night
- Read something inspiring or educational
- Journal your thoughts and experiences
- Learn something new every day

Body

- Stretch or do yoga: Morning and night
- ♀ Exercise or go for a walk
- Start the day with lemon water
- Drink at least 2L of water
- Eat nourishing, home-cooked meals
- Get 15 minutes of sunshine
- Take a cold shower (if you're feeling adventurous!)

Soul

- Meditate or engage in a spiritual practice
- Be creative or enter a flow state
- Explore gratitude and mindfulness
- Try a new hobby or activity
- Spend quality time with loved ones
- Connect with nature

Part 2

BUILDING THE TRINITY

Chapter 5

Gratitude:
The Unsung Superpower

> **Gratitude is not only the greatest of virtues but the parent of all others."**
>
> *– Cicero*

Imagine you have just finished a long, tiring day. You collapse on the couch, scrolling mindlessly through social media, when suddenly it hits you: life isn't *all* bad. That barista who gave you extra foam on your latte? That funny text message your friend sent. Your cat choosing *not* to knock over your coffee for once? Those little things, which mostly go unnoticed, are the unsung heroes of your day. That's gratitude—a deceptively simple but profoundly transformative superpower.

How Gratitude Grounds Us

Gratitude works similarly to the best friend who is always there to remind you when you act loony and are too arrogant for your own good. It is the part where we go, "Hey, life, I see your chaos, but I also see your gifts."

It works because:

- **It anchors us in the present:** When you focus on what you're grateful for, you stop time-traveling to past regrets or future anxieties.

- **It rewires your brain for positivity:** Studies show that consistent gratitude practice can literally shift your brain's wiring, making you more attuned to the good stuff.

Gratitude can be described as the filter through which one views life. Without it, minor disturbances—such as spilling coffee on your shirt, for example—turn into disasters. With it, that same spill becomes a reminder: *I own a washing machine. Life's still good.*

The Ripple Effect of Gratitude

Gratitude doesn't just make you feel warm and fuzzy; it's contagious. Imagine this:

You're at your local coffee shop, running late, but instead of rushing off, you pause to thank the barista:

- *"Hey, thanks for always being so cheerful—it really makes my mornings brighter!"*
The barista beams, feeling seen and appreciated. Later, she compliments a customer's scarf, who then holds the door for someone else. By lunchtime, half the city is smiling because you started a chain reaction of good vibes.

Exercises to Harness Gratitude

1. **Keep a Gratitude Journal:**
   At the end of each day, write down three things you're grateful for. No need to overthink—write anything from "I didn't burn dinner" to "My boss actually said thank you today." Bonus: On tough days, you can revisit these gems and remember that not every day was a dumpster fire.

   Humorous Example:

   - Grateful my pants still fit after that third cookie.

   - Grateful my coworker shared Wi-Fi passwords instead of drama.

   - Grateful my dog finally learned "sit" (well, *kind of*).

2. **The Thank-You Challenge:**
   Every day, thank one person sincerely. Could be the grocery store clerk, a teammate at work, or even your mom (who probably deserves a *lot* more thanks).

   Real-Life Moment:
   I once thanked my Uber driver for navigating through traffic with ninja-like precision. He smiled and said, "You're the first rider to ever thank me." By the end of the ride, we were joking about potholes like old pals.

3. **Gratitude Walks:**
   While walking (to clear your mind or escape your roommate's karaoke practice), actively notice things to be grateful for—chirping birds, blue

skies, or even that one leaf clinging bravely to a tree in winter.

The Humor in Gratitude

Let's face it: gratitude isn't always glamorous.

- There are days when the best you can muster is, "I'm grateful I didn't accidentally forward a sarcastic text to the person I was speaking ill of."

- Or "I'm grateful for the stretch pants because holiday cookies happened."

The point is gratitude doesn't demand perfection or doesn't require you to pretend. It's about finding light in the little things, even when life feels like it's auditioning for a disaster movie.

Final Thought: The Hidden Power

Gratitude may seem like a simple practice, but its effects are profound. It's not about ignoring life's challenges but about recognizing the little joys that often go unnoticed. Gratitude shifts our perspective, turning what we have into enough and the difficult moments into opportunities for growth. It's about seeing the silver linings that exist even when things aren't perfect.

Gratitude teaches us to value the little things—like a thoughtful message from a friend or a warm cup of coffee in the morning. It enables us to make failures into a positive aspect demonstrating to us that it is always possible to learn from that failure. When you carry out what gratitude entails, you do not lessen the sad times in life but instead look at those as part of life too.

And as a last resort, count your blessings, the trivialities which people take for granted most of the time. Like getting Wi-Fi that works or pizza that provides satisfaction or a phone that lasts when it falls.

Gratitude, no matter how trivial it may seem, is powerful in its ability to bring us back to what matters. As the saying goes, "Gratitude unlocks the fullness of life"—or, if you prefer, "Gratitude unlocks the fullness of wine glasses." Cheers to that!

Chapter 6
Nurturing the Body

> **" Take care of your body. It's the only place you have to live."**
>
> — *Jim Rohn*

Now, the body – a reliable friend, despite some rust and squeaking that occur over the course of our journey called life. This is your life car, your mode of transport for the longest time possible, so ensure you get the best. I mean you do not neglect your car by not changing the car oil or driving on worn out tires (unless it involves a car chase), why do that to your body? Taking care of your body is about maintaining this amazing vehicle so you can live and do so to optimal capacity. And, after all, as it has been said, when the body is satisfied, the mind and the soul take the same position as personal backup dancers.

Exercise: Moving Your Way to Joy

Let's start with exercise. Don't roll your eyes just yet and think '*Oh great, another rant about the gym memberships*', hear me out. Exercise does not necessarily have to be torturing oneself with burpees or running marathon. It's about how you feel while dancing to your favorite song in the living room or walking and running after your dog – even if the dog outruns you.

For instance, my cousin Ritu was against the gym and never wanted to go to the gym at all. She would register every January, attend twice, and then engage in a vibrant fabricated denial of treadmills for the other eleven months. Forcing oneself to ride a bicycle was hard but one day her friend forced her to join Zumba dance class. Ritu liked it—not because she could dance well (which she obviously couldn't). The key is finding an activity that doesn't feel like a chore but like a reward.

The benefits of exercise go beyond toned abs (though those are nice too). Burden of duties can put lots of pressure especially on the emotional well-being of a person, but movement helps lift your mood, free your mind, and gives the soul some dance of joy. And it's also a nice reality check, like my Pilates instructor once told me, 'Your body is more than just a hanger for clothes—it's a powerhouse that deserves love and care'.

Nutrition: The Art of Eating (and Actually Enjoying It)

Next up: food. Let me make this clear to you - if you thought that eating healthy and taking care of your body required you to give up chocolate or drink only kale smoothies, then sorry to disappoint you. Life's too short to eat things that taste like cardboard. Nutrition is about balance, not deprivation.

Take my friend Arjun. He had previously abused his body like that of a non-biodegradable dustbin and ate whatever that is fast, cheap that came in a paper bag. He would lack the energy, he would also feel irritable, and always sleepy. He wakes one day, after a particularly vicious cold that laid him out for weeks was severe enough that he began to adjust. He gave up the daily dose of a sweet cereal in the morning and had a big portion of oatmeal instead, included more vegetables to his dinner and increased his water intake. The result? It wasn't just that Arjun's body was strong – he was stronger in mind and soul as well.

The lesson? Food is fuel, not filler. The idea is to have a colorful plate (and by that we don't mean a bag of Skittles). That means lean proteins, whole grain, healthy fat, and plenty of fresh fruits and vegetables. But also, don't avoid the occasional slice of pizza or a scoop of ice cream. A nurtured body is one that feels both nourished and satisfied.

Rest: The Secret Ingredient You're Probably Ignoring

Now let's go over what might be the most important but overlooked aspect of being physically healthy: rest. The truth is that even in a society that extols productivity and being busy, sleep and other forms of rest receive very little regard. But here's the truth: rest isn't lazy—it's essential.

Take my unfortunate aunt Shanti for instance she learnt this the hard way. For years she literally worked till the lamp post, skipping sleep, and surviving on caffeine alone. One day her body decided it would no longer tolerate such treatment: she fainted during a meeting. Thus, she perceived her body is not a machine and needs to rest after a terrifying visit to the hospital. Now, Shanti prioritizes sleep, takes short naps when she's tired, and even treats herself to the occasional lazy Sunday.

It's not just about sleep (although, aiming for 7-8 hours of sound sleep is a good first step). It's also about becoming okay with taking breaks—a cup of coffee with a book, a walk in a park, or even just sitting and gazing out the window. At that time your body heals, your spirit relaxes, and your soul breathes a little easier.

The Body-Mind-Soul Connection

Here's the kicker: when you nurture your body, you're not just helping yourself physically. A healthy body sends positive ripples through your entire being. Exercise floods your brain with endorphins, making you feel happier. Eating well fuels your mind, helping you focus and think clearly. And rest? It gives you the energy to pursue the things that feed your soul.

Think of it this way: your body is the soil where your mind and soul grow. If the soil is dry, cracked, and neglected, nothing thrives. But when it's well-tended, everything flourishes.

The Humor in Staying Healthy

Of course, nurturing your body isn't always glamorous. You'll have days when your workout feels like a death march, or when your attempt at a "healthy" meal turns into a Pinterest fail. You might even find yourself falling asleep mid-meditation or accidentally eating an entire bag of chips while watching TV (hey, we've all been there).

The good news? You don't have to be perfect. Your body doesn't demand perfection—it just wants consistency, kindness, and a little effort. Laugh at the missteps and keep going.

Actionable Tips for a Healthy Body

- **Move Daily:** Aim for at least 30 minutes of activity most days but pick something you enjoy so it doesn't feel like a chore.

- **Eat Intentionally:** Focus on whole, nutritious foods, but allow yourself indulgences without guilt. Moderation is key.

- **Hydrate:** Drink water like it's your job. Your body (and skin) will thank you.

- **Sleep Well:** Create a bedtime routine, avoid screens before bed, and prioritize getting enough sleep.

- **Listen to Your Body:** If it's tired, rest. If it's hungry, eat. If it's craving movement, get up and stretch.

A Final Thought

As huge as your body may be to house your spirit and soul, how can it be that it is not more than a tool to use in this great tapestry of living? When you cultivate it, you are helping the physical body to regain its strength, yet at the same time, laying the foundations to emotional and spiritual well-being. Each glass of water you consume, each vegetable you incorporate in your plate, each stretch you make is an act of love towards the body.

You need to consider your body is your friend for a lifetime – one that communicates its needs in subtle ways. Listening to those cues is the ultimate form of self-respect. When you feel tired, rest. When you're energized, move. By acknowledging all these signals, one establishes a positive relationship with own body.

Lastly, it is eminently important not to forget that perfection isn't the goal—progress is. A nurtured body does not require perfect sessions at the gym or perfect diet that is fit for the post on Instagram. It thrives with Practice, Tolerance and Thinking kindly to yourself occasionally, yes it flourishes best on those aspects. Every move you make is a vote for a better you and much improved health and well-being.

Hence consider the body as the precious asset that it is. Transition it happily, maintain it purposefully, and sleep it gracefully. In return, it will support you in life, safeguard you and help you stay healthy far into your senior years. After all, a nurtured body is not just the foundation of health—it's the birthplace of happiness, radiance, and endless possibilities.

Chapter 7
Mastering the Mind

> **"** The mind is a powerful thing.
> It can take you through walls."
>
> *– Denis Avey*

If your body is the foundation and your soul is the essence, then your mind is the control center—a complex, quirky operator running the show It reasons, gets jealous, angry, happy, Neuro transmits and receives information, yes it fantasizes and at 3 am it chooses to remind you of a moment 10 years ago that you considered embarrassing. Managing your thoughts is like getting a new software for your phone – not just does things runs better; it unlocks potential you didn't know you had.

But here's the catch: even though the mind is strong-willed it can also be very demanding. Sustained stress, interruptions and doubting your abilities can take control over it and create a situation when instead of a precise compass pointing you in the right direction, it all becomes a noisy backseat driver. The good news? It is possible to learn how to control your mind and make it work for you instead of against you in just some time if you have the right instruments.

Stress Management: Taming the Inner Drama Queen

Let's begin with stress—because if your mind were a character in a soap opera, stress would be its overacting nemesis. The bills! The deadlines! The "seen" message on WhatsApp with no reply! Left unchecked, stress can take over, leaving your mind stuck in fight-or-flight mode.

My friend Priya has constantly ongoing mental traffic congestion. The discovery of deep breathing brought peace to her life when she stopped being tense and stopped thinking too much. According to her she found this initially bizarre. Stress is present in every breath as I continue inhaling and exhaling. She attempted the exercise by taking controlled breaths that lasted for both inward and outward movement of air. Her mental confusion vanished for a moment while she felt remarkably calm.

Other stress relieving techniques include mindfulness meditation (think of it as a spa day for your brain) and physical movement (exercise flushes stress hormones right out of your system). Even something as simple as taking a break—stepping outside, listening to music, or chatting with a friend—can reset your mental state.

Focus: Finding Clarity in the Noise

Ever tried to concentrate but found your mind wandering to what you'll have for dinner, whether penguins have knees, or if you locked the front door? Congratulations, you're human. However, in a world where all around us we can hear ringing, notifications, and other distractions, concentrating is an Olympic feat.

Enter **goal-setting**—your mind's best friend. When you give your brain a clear target, it stops fooling around and gets to work. My cousin Ravi (yes, him again!) swears by his "three things rule": each morning, he writes down the three most important tasks for the day. Just three. By focusing on these, he avoids the overwhelm of a never-ending to-do list and ends the day with a sense of achievement.

Another trick? The **Pomodoro Technique**. Work for 25 minutes, then take a 5-minute break. It's like bribing your brain: "Focus now, and you get a prize later." And as for those disruptions – turn off the notifications, declutter the environment, if needed, put the phone in another room.

Creativity: Unlocking Your Inner Genius

Creativity doesn't belong only to creativity gurus who create great paintings and great literature; creativity belongs to everyone. It's what you use to reason, to be creative and to find another way to put the fun in life. But let's be real: there are days when the idea seems to be about as attainable as the internet signal on a hilltop.

That's where **journaling** comes in handy Writing is not only therapeutic, but it is the sandbox of your mind. My friend Meera calls her journal her "idea incubator." She writes whatever comes to her, be it dreams she may have or ideas that are still in the conception and then takes time to see what may work.

Meditation can also spark creativity. This means that when you empty your mind, you make a channel that allows new thoughts into your mind. And if you can't find anything, just do something that's not related to the problem you're trying to solve – go for a walk, play a game, doodle something on a piece of paper. Sometimes, that extra distance allows your subconscious to do the connecting that your conscious mind could not.

Techniques to Master the Mind

Here are some actionable ways to turn your mind into your greatest ally:

1. **Meditation:** Give 10 minutes of your day to practice mindfulness. It's that simple: just do not complicate the exercise, sit, bring your attention to the fact that you are breathing right now.

2. **Journaling:** Start a gratitude journal, jot down your thoughts, or brainstorm ideas. Writing helps untangle the mental spaghetti.

3. **Goal setting:** Achieving colossal goals must be done through tiny obtainable and easily manageable targets. This can be achieved through things such as a checklist, a vision board, utilizing an application or perhaps a calendar.

4. **Breaks:** Don't underestimate the power of rest. Work in focused bursts and reward yourself with short breaks.

5. **Positive Affirmations:** Remind yourself of your strengths. Say it out loud: "I am capable, creative, and in control." It feels cheesy, but it works.

6. **Laugh:** Yes, really. Watch a comedy, call a funny friend, or just laugh at the absurdity of life. Humor resets your brain like nothing else.

The Humor in Mastering the Mind

Of course, mastering your mind isn't always smooth sailing. You'll meditate and realize you've spent the entire session thinking about groceries. You'll journal and write, "What even is life?" followed by a doodle of a sad potato. You'll set goals, only to procrastinate with a "quick" YouTube video that turns into a three-hour binge.

But that's part of the journey. Your mind isn't a machine—it's a quirky, unpredictable masterpiece. Treat it with patience, kindness, and a dash of humor, and it will reward you with clarity, focus, and creativity.

A Final Thought

It is the thoughts of your head that you oversee the vessel that is your life. This means that when the flow is stressed, distracted or chaotic, the entire ship wobbles. But when it's clear, calm, and creative, it is your compass during any storm; it ensures you find direction through challenges; ensure you make the right decisions and reach your goals with direction and confidence.

Control of the mind isn't a process of striving to achieve positive or negative outcomes or complete control. And what it means is achieving the balance between your mind, your heart, and your steps. It is having a right state of mental health to enable one to handle life issues in a stable manner. This helps you see themes in how you behave, change negative thought processes to more positive and develop behaviors that can aid in reaching your objectives.

Mind feeding is a lifelong process which means that one must constantly monitor his or her mental health, learn when to take rest or seek a healthy rejuvenation methodology. From meditations, journaling to making a shift in your mindset, these skills work towards making you an observer of your own mind. Slowly and gradually, this fosters one's emotional intelligence and in turn helps in one's personal and interpersonal relationships.

Ultimately, controlling the mind is much more than only being able to control stress or pay attention. It is fundamentally about starting a relationship with yourself that is as good and as solid as possible. The better you comprehend and nurture your psyche, the better it will nurture you – in intellect, imagination, and insight across all your endeavors. With each other, you and your mind can take on whatever life has to offer you boldly, elegantly, and – always – with a bit of laughter.

Techniques to Master the Mind – In Depth

Mastering your mind is about turning it from a chaotic control tower into a calm, strategic navigator. Here's a closer look at techniques that can help you manage stress, focus better, and unleash creativity.

1. Meditation: The Art of Sitting Still (and Not Falling Asleep)

Meditation isn't about shutting off your thoughts (seriously, who can do that?). It's about observing them without judgment. Think of it as mental housekeeping—sweeping away clutter to make room for clarity.

- **How to Meditate:**
    - ☐ Find a quiet space where you won't be disturbed (yes, even the bathroom works in a pinch).

- ☐ Sit comfortably, close your eyes, and focus on your breath. Inhale slowly, exhale even slower.

- ☐ Your mind will wander—guaranteed. When it does, gently guide it back to your breath.

- ☐ Start with 5-10 minutes a day and work your way up.

- **Benefits:** Meditation reduces stress by calming your nervous system, enhances focus, and boosts creativity. It's like giving your brain a mini spa day.

- **Pro Tip:** Apps like Headspace or Insight Timer can be great for beginners.

2. Journaling: Putting Your Thoughts on Paper

Journaling is like having a conversation with yourself—only quieter and less awkward. It helps you process emotions, organize your thoughts, and unleash creativity.

- **How to Journal:**

  - ☐ **Gratitude Journal:** The journal demands you note three daily grateful events. The practice enables you to concentrate on your positive experiences.

  - ☐ **Brain Dump:** Feeling overwhelmed? Take note of whatever comes to mind regardless of its nonsensical nature. It clears mental clutter.

  - ☐ **Reflection Journal:** Reflect on your day. What went well? What could have gone better? What did you learn?

- **Benefits:** Journaling helps manage stress, improve emotional intelligence, and spark creative ideas. Plus, it's cheaper than therapy.

- **Pro Tip:** The primary rule for journaling is to ignore matters of structure and grammar. This isn't your 10th-grade English assignment.

3. Goal setting: Giving Your Mind a Mission

Your mind loves having something to work toward. Goal setting channels your mental energy into something productive, reducing the likelihood of overthinking or getting distracted by cat videos.

- **How to Set Goals:**
  - ☐ Use the **SMART Framework** (Specific, Measurable, Achievable, Relevant, Time-bound).
  - ☐ Break big goals into smaller, manageable steps. For example, "Write a book" becomes "Write 500 words a day."
  - ☐ Regularly review your progress and adjust as needed.

- **Benefits:** Setting goals gives your mind purpose, boosts motivation, and builds confidence as you achieve them.

- **Pro Tip:** Write your goals down. Studies show you're more likely to achieve them when they're on paper (or in a note on your phone).

4. Breaks: The Secret Sauce for Productivity

Contrary to what hustle culture tells you, taking breaks isn't slacking—it's smart. Your brain isn't designed to focus for hours on end.

- **How to Take Effective Breaks:**

  ☐ Use the **Pomodoro Technique**: Work for 25 minutes, then take a 5-minute break. After four sessions, take a longer break (15-30 minutes).

  ☐ During breaks, step away from your workspace. Stretch, drink water, or stare out the window like a brooding philosopher.

- **Benefits:** Breaks improve focus, reduce stress, and prevent burnout. Think of them as mental fuel stops.

- **Pro Tip:** Avoid using breaks to scroll social media—it's a focus killer. Instead, try a quick walk or a few deep breaths.

5. Positive Affirmations: Flipping the Mental Script

Your mind believes what you tell it. Positive affirmations rewire your thought patterns, replacing negativity with empowering beliefs.

- **How to Use Affirmations:**

  ☐ Choose affirmations that resonate with you, like "I am capable" or "I can handle whatever comes my way."

  ☐ Say them aloud in front of a mirror, write them down, or repeat them silently during meditation.

- **Benefits:** Affirmations boost self-confidence, reduce self-doubt, and help you maintain a positive mindset.

- **Pro Tip:** Pair affirmations with action. For example, if you say, "I am healthy," take steps to support that belief, like eating well or exercising.

6. Laughter: The Ultimate Mind Reset

It's impossible to stay stressed when you're laughing. Laughter releases endorphins (your brain's happy chemicals) and reduces stress hormones.

- **How to Add More Laughter to Your Day:**

  - ☐ Watch a funny video, listen to a comedy podcast, or hang out with friends who crack you up.

  - ☐ Don't take yourself too seriously—learn to laugh at your own mistakes (like the time you wore mismatched socks to a meeting).

- **Benefits:** Laughter improves mood, enhances creativity, and gives your mind a much-needed reset.

- **Pro Tip:** Keep a collection of go-to jokes, memes, or videos for when you need a quick pick-me-up.

Final Thoughts on Techniques

To master your mind, one must focus on advancement instead of perfection. Three tools of meditation bring clarity while journaling systems difficult thoughts and goal setting provides proper guidance. Between breaks and laughter, the mind stays relaxed, and affirmations help you remember your strength.

Start small. Two mental techniques are sufficient to establish a daily practice. As time advances your mind will stop running wild and transform into a dependable directional tool which leads you towards balanced approaches to fulfillment. Any moment of instability sends you off course (which will happen), so you simply laugh about it before you reset and repeat your efforts. Mastery demands continuous effort since it requires development above everything else.

Chapter 8
Awakening the Soul

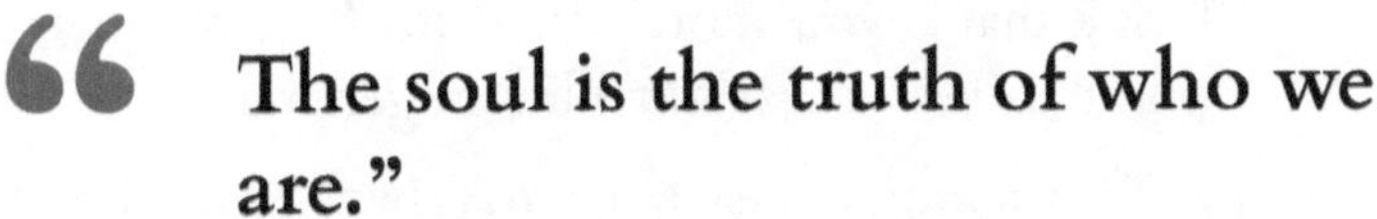

The soul is the truth of who we are."

– Marianne Williamson

The soul acts as a guiding lighthouse which helps us find our purpose as it brings light and stability in the most challenging life waters. The process of awakening your soul requires you to eliminate distractions to rediscover the inner truth which has never left you but was hidden under distracting noise. Inside each of us exists an inner voice which reveals that existence holds greater value than work tasks and scheduling.

The soul stands fairly reserved in its nature. Being neglectful to the soul makes life meaningless because it is like viewing a breathtaking film without audio. People discover profound purpose through recognizing their soul through appreciation or spiritual prayer and natural world connection as well as social bonds with others.

Gratitude: The Soul's Vitamin D

Gratitude is like sunlight for your soul—it warms it, energizes it, and helps it grow. When you focus on what you're thankful for, you shift your perspective from scarcity to abundance. Suddenly, life feels richer, even if nothing external has changed.

- **How to Practice Gratitude:**

  - ☐ Keep a gratitude journal. Each night, jot down three things you're grateful for—big or small. (Yes, "pizza" counts!)

  - ☐ Say thank you more often, not just to others but also to yourself and life in general.

  - ☐ Take a moment each day to reflect on the good things—like a kind word, a stunning sunset, or the fact that you didn't burn your toast this morning.

- **Benefits:** Gratitude helps you feel more connected to the present moment, reduces stress, and strengthens your relationships. It's like a soul hug.

- **Pro Tip:** Struggling to find something to be grateful for? Start small. "I'm grateful for coffee" is just as valid as "I'm grateful for world peace."

Prayer: A Conversation with the Universe

Prayer isn't just for Sunday mornings or specific religions—it's a universal way of connecting with something bigger than yourself. It's less about asking for stuff (no, a new car probably isn't on the menu) and more about building a relationship with the divine, the universe, or whatever higher power you believe in.

- **How to Pray:**

  - ☐ There's no "right" way. Speak from the heart, whether it's in words, thoughts, or silence.

  - ☐ You can pray for guidance, express gratitude, or simply share your thoughts.

- ☐ Set aside a quiet moment each day—before bed, during a walk, or even in the car (just don't close your eyes if you're driving).

- **Benefits:** Prayer fosters a sense of peace, hope, and connection. It's like sending a love letter to the cosmos.

- **Pro Tip:** Not religious? Try affirmations or mindful reflection instead. The goal is the same: to connect with your inner essence.

Connecting with Nature: Recharging the Soul's Battery

Nature is the ultimate soul healer. There's something magical about standing beneath a vast sky, listening to the rustle of leaves, or feeling the earth beneath your feet. It reminds you that you're part of something much larger—and it's incredibly humbling.

- **How to Connect with Nature:**
  - ☐ Go for a walk in the park, sit by a river, or hike up a hill.
  - ☐ Practice *earthing*—walking barefoot on grass or sand to feel grounded.
  - ☐ Pause to appreciate the little things: the chirping of birds, the smell of rain, the patterns of clouds.

- **Benefits:** Time in nature reduces stress, boosts creativity, and gives you a sense of awe and wonder. It's like therapy, but free.

- **Pro Tip:** Make it a habit. Even 10 minutes a day outdoors can work wonders for your soul.

Fostering Community: The Soul's Favorite Place to Be

Humans are wired for connection. While the soul thrives in moments of solitude, it also craves the warmth of community—a sense of belonging that reminds you, "You're not alone." Whether it's family, friends, or a shared group, community is where the soul feels most alive.

- **How to Build Community:**
    - ☐ Join a group that shares your interests—like a book club, yoga class, or volunteer organization.
    - ☐ Be present with the people around you. Listen deeply, share openly, and create meaningful moments.
    - ☐ Celebrate together, whether it's a birthday, a festival, or just making it through the week.
- **Benefits:** Community gives you support, shared joy, and a sense of purpose. It's like soul food—nourishing and satisfying.
- **Pro Tip:** Don't wait for community to find you—create it. Host a potluck, plan a game night, or simply reach out to someone for coffee.

The Humor in Awakening the Soul

Of course, soul-awakening practices don't always go as planned. You'll start a gratitude journal only to realize you've written "coffee" every day for a week. You'll head into nature for peace and quiet, only to encounter a mosquito army. And you'll try prayer, only to spend half the time wondering if you left the stove on.

But that's okay. Awakening the soul isn't about perfection; it's about presence. The more you practice, the more you'll notice those small, soulful moments that make life rich and meaningful.

A Final Thought

A personal spiritual experience requires attentive listening to the potent yet soft-hearted messages as opposed to passive waiting for a significant life change. A soul embraces simple pleasures because true connection with present moments brings its maximum happiness. These little seemingly ordinary occurrences of a cup of tea enjoyment and a hug embrace and a sunset display combine to show the soul how to focus on essential matters.

Human activity leads us to neglect listening to our inner voice although we do it frequently. Creating room for thankfulness together with earnest supplication alongside encounters with nature along with community participation activates our genuine self-discovery. This connection serves as our spiritual compass that leads our lives directly and clears our path with goal direction and inner serenity.

So, take a moment to reconnect with your soul today. A basic connection with your inner self is achievable with any straightforward practice from deep breathing to expressing gratitude to taking a nature walk. Your journey toward soul-building will naturally guide you toward obtaining the wisdom and peaceful state which dwells within your essence. The soul's awakening leads to a life experience that becomes simpler and filled with more joy. Within such a domain every aspect takes on an elevated purpose while appearing somewhat brighter.

Part 3

HARMONY IN PRACTICE

Chapter 9
The Dance of the Trinity

> " When you dance, your purpose is not to get to a certain place on the floor. It's to enjoy each step along the way."
>
> *– Wayne Dyer*

Picture this: your body, mind, and soul as three wildly different but equally passionate dance partners. The body's got rhythm, the mind is choreographing like it's auditioning for *So You Think You Can Dance*, and the soul. Oh, the soul's out there twirling like nobody's watching. When they're in sync, it's a masterpiece. But when one trips, it's like watching a penguin try salsa—chaotic but oddly endearing.

This chapter explores how these three elements groove together, what happens when they get out of step, and how to keep the dance floor smooth—even when life decides to spill its drink on it.

The Body: The Rhythm Keeper

The body is the reliable drummer of this trio, keeping the beat steady (most of the time). But if you ignore it— skipping meals, pulling all-nighters, or treating coffee as a food group—it'll strike back faster than a hangry toddler.

- **How the Body Influences the Mind:**

  ☐ A healthy, active body sharpens the mind like a well-honed pencil. Exercise is basically your brain's version of hitting the refresh button.

  ☐ Neglect the body, though, and welcome brain fog, grumpiness, and the sudden urge to fight the next person who breathes too loudly.

- **How the Body Influences the Soul:**

  ☐ Ever gone for a walk and felt like you suddenly understand the meaning of life—or at least where you left your car keys? That's your body handing the mic to your soul.

  ☐ On the flip side, an aching body makes even the happiest soul grumble, "Why stairs? Why me?"

The Mind: The Choreographer

The mind is the overachieving director, planning every move, cue, and step. When it's calm and focused, everything flows. But when it's stressed, it's like a toddler with a whistle—chaos, noise, and questionable decisions.

- **How the Mind Influences the Body:**

  ☐ Positive thoughts lead to actions that nurture your body. It's the mind saying, "Eat your veggies," and you begrudgingly agreeing.

  ☐ An anxious mind, however, can turn a small headache into a dramatic WebMD deep dive that ends with you convinced it's something rare and unpronounceable.

- How the Mind Influences the Soul:

  - ☐ A calm mind creates space for reflection, inspiration, and the kind of soul-level epiphanies that usually involve a sunset or a really good cup of tea.

  - ☐ A cluttered mind? It's like static on the radio—you can't hear the song over all the noise.

The Soul: The Melody

The soul is the heart and essence of the trinity, the melody that gives life its depth, richness, and purpose. While the body keeps the beat and the mind choreographs the moves, the soul is the "why" behind it all—the invisible thread tying everything together. It's the part of you that seeks meaning, connection, and joy, turning the dance from a series of steps into an art form.

However, the soul is sensitive and unyielding when ignored. Neglect it for too long, and it won't hesitate to sulk in the metaphorical corner, arms crossed, glaring at the mind and body for their lack of attention. When nurtured, though, the soul becomes the source of inspiration and fulfillment that fuels every other aspect of your being.

How the Soul Influences the Mind:

- A connected soul acts as the mind's compass, providing clarity and purpose. When your soul is in tune, it gives your thoughts direction, guiding you toward decisions and actions that align with your values and aspirations. It's like having an internal GPS gently reminding you of your true path—

even if it occasionally chirps, "Recalculating…" when life throws you off course.

- On the flip side, a neglected soul leaves the mind in a state of restlessness and confusion. Without that inner connection, the mind may spiral into overthinking, doubt, and existential questions like, "What's the point of all this?" It's the mental equivalent of driving aimlessly without a map, frustrated and unsure where you're headed.

How the Soul Influences the Body:

- When the soul is happy and nourished, even the simplest activities feel imbued with purpose. Folding laundry, cooking a meal, or taking a walk can suddenly seem like acts of mindfulness and gratitude. This is when your soul whispers, "There's beauty even in the ordinary," making every movement feel meaningful and intentional. (Yes, Marie Kondo's philosophy of sparking joy applies here too!)

- But when the soul is out of sync, it casts a shadow over the body's energy. Tasks that should feel light and enjoyable—like dancing or exercising—become burdensome, as though you're wading through wet cement. The body may move, but without the soul's melody, it feels like going through the motions without any real rhythm or joy.

The soul, then, is the unspoken music of your life. It doesn't demand much—just your attention, a moment of quiet, or a connection to something greater than yourself. When you honor it, it rewards you with a sense of harmony that elevates both the body and the mind, turning the everyday dance of life into a deeply meaningful and beautiful performance.

Practical Strategies to Keep the Dance Alive

1. Daily Check-Ins:

- Ask yourself:
    - ☐ Is my body energized, or does it feel like it ran a marathon (without running one)?
    - ☐ Is my mind clear, or is it busy planning imaginary arguments in the shower?
    - ☐ Does my soul feel connected, or is it sulking in the metaphorical break room?

2. Holistic Habits:

- Combine routines for a triple win:
    - ☐ Morning yoga? Body: check. Mind: check. Soul: check. Plus, you can feel smug about it all day.

3. Mindful Adjustments:

- When one element is struggling:
    - ☐ Tired body? Nap without guilt (even if it's just closing your eyes and pretending to meditate).
    - ☐ Overwhelmed mind? Write a to-do list—or doodle on it until it feels less scary.
    - ☐ Disconnected soul? Pet a dog, hug a tree, or do whatever quirky thing makes your spirit say, "Ah, that's better."

4. Scheduled Practices:

- Plan time for each partner:

  - ☐ Mondays: Move your body (preferably not just to the fridge).

  - ☐ Wednesdays: Feed your mind with something other than gossip.

  - ☐ Sundays: Let your soul take the wheel—it's usually wiser than you think.

5. Celebrate Harmony:

  - ☐ Did you manage a workout, finish a book, or meditate without falling asleep? Celebrate it! Bonus points if you do all three in one day—you're practically a wellness wizard.

The Humor in the Dance

It is no joke when we mention the "Dance of the Trinity" because this performance more closely resembles a clumsy slapstick routine rather than a traditional dance performance. The demands between your body that craves sleep, and your mind occupied with deadlines push your soul to what state? It's in the corner screaming, "Can we PLEASE go to the beach?!"

Along your route toward success life suddenly appears to sabotage you. Maybe your yoga flow gets interrupted by a toddler asking about dinosaurs. Or you burn dinner while "feeding your soul" with karaoke. The key? Laugh it off. Nothing kills the vibe faster than taking it all too seriously.

A Final Thought

The dance of the trinity—your body, mind, and soul—isn't a performance to be perfected or judged. It's a journey, a rhythm of life that evolves with every step, stumble, and sway. There will be days when the trio moves in perfect harmony, creating a masterpiece that feels effortless and deeply fulfilling. On other days, the rhythm will falter, and it may feel like you're awkwardly shuffling across the dance floor, unsure of your next move.

And that's okay. The beauty of this dance isn't in getting it "right" every time but in showing up, staying in motion, and being willing to adapt to the music of life as it changes. Each misstep is a chance to learn, each pause an opportunity to reset, and each breakthrough a reminder of how powerful it is when all three elements—body, mind, and soul—work together.

The secret isn't in perfection; it's in persistence. It's in finding joy in the process, even when life throws unexpected challenges your way. Maybe your body feels tired, your mind is frazzled, or your soul feels distant. In those moments, the answer isn't to stop dancing—it's to tune in, adjust, and let one part of the trinity support the others until they're ready to rejoin the rhythm.

The dance floor always remains available for anyone who wants to join. Regardless of how you dance through life which may involve peace or complexity or chaos you remain in motion. You're still growing. Through movement you bring forth your original dance style.

Live with acceptance of imperfect moments and enjoy the moments of failure and rejoice when achieving minor achievements. The trinity dance demonstrates a lifestyle approach which teaches us that existence focuses on binding relationships more than it does on flawless management and joy.

Now, go ahead. Grab your imaginary dancing shoes while forgetting performance expectations so you can immerse yourself completely in the melodies that make up your existence. The beginning of each successful dance venture requires both initial bravery for the first few steps as well as continuous momentum regardless of the circumstances.

Chapter 10
Embracing Gratitude Daily

" Enjoy the little things, for one day you may look back and realize they were the big things."

– Robert Brault

Gratitude isn't just a warm, fuzzy feeling you pull out on Thanksgiving—it's a daily practice, a life-enhancing habit, and sometimes, the only thing standing between you and a meltdown over a slow Wi-Fi connection. Gratitude is like the multi-vitamin for your soul: you may not always notice its effects right away, but over time, it builds resilience, boosts positivity, and makes life a little shinier.

The Magic of Everyday Gratitude

When gratitude becomes part of your daily routine, it transforms the mundane into the meaningful. You start seeing beauty in little things, like a stranger holding the door for you, your favorite song playing on the radio, or finally finding a matching pair of socks in the laundry pile. It's a simple shift in perspective that can make even the most ordinary Tuesday feel like a celebration.

Think about it—when was the last time you paused to appreciate that first sip of coffee in the morning or the fact that your phone didn't autocorrect "love you" to "leave you" in a text? These small moments, when noticed and cherished, create a ripple effect of positivity throughout your day.

Gratitude as a Quirk-Friendly Practice

Let's not pretend gratitude always must be profound. Sometimes, it's about celebrating the downright quirky blessings in life. Like that one time you made it through an entire Zoom call without saying, "You're on mute!" Or the sheer joy of realizing the office microwave *didn't* leave your leftovers smelling like someone else's fish curry.

One of my favorite gratitude moments? A friend of mine was having a rough day and decided to focus on the silver linings. She ended up genuinely grateful for her dog's ability to "accidentally" interrupt her work calls by barking at imaginary squirrels. "At least someone's got my back," she said.

Practical Tips for Cultivating Gratitude

1. **Start a Gratitude Journal:**
   Jot down three things you're grateful for every day. They don't have to be life-changing— "I didn't spill coffee on my shirt today" totally counts.

2. **Thank Someone Daily:**
   Make it a habit to thank someone, whether it's the barista who gets your order just right or a coworker who shares memes that keep you sane during deadlines.

3. **Gratitude Walks:**
    Take a walk and mentally list things you're thankful for. Bonus points if you can do it without tripping over a crack in the sidewalk while admiring the trees.

4. **Celebrate Small Wins:**
    Did you finally clear your inbox? Found a parking spot close to the store? Managed not to burn dinner? Give yourself a mini high-five.

The Humor in Everyday Gratitude

Gratitude has a way of sneaking into the most unexpected places, and let's face it, sometimes it's downright hilarious. Like when you're grateful for your Wi-Fi working perfectly—right until you realize you've been connected to your neighbor's network all week. Or when you thank your partner for washing the dishes, only to discover they "washed" them by shoving them in the dishwasher without hitting start.

Life is full of these little ironies, and gratitude is the best way to turn them into laughter instead of frustration. After all, what's the point of getting worked up over a burnt piece of toast when you can just scrape it off, call it "extra crunchy," and be thankful for the invention of toasters?

Final Thought: Gratitude as a Daily Superpower

Gratitude functions as more than a passing emotion because it represents a deliberate decision and psychological orientation which makes ordinary situations meaningful.

Thankfully a cup of gratitude serves as a prevention against stress that functions as both a mood rehab tool and protects individuals during technical disruption.

The beauty of gratitude lies in its simplicity. It doesn't require grand gestures or life-changing events. It thrives in the little things—the way the sun filters through your window in the morning, the laughter shared over a silly joke, the comfort of a well-worn hoodie, or the first sip of coffee that just *hits right.* It's in the small victories, like remembering where you put your keys, catching the green light when you're running late, or finally clearing your inbox (even if it lasts only five minutes).

When you make gratitude a daily habit, you begin to see life differently. It shifts your focus from what's missing to what's already there. You learn to notice valuable things in any situation —a warm gesture of a random person or songs expressing positive memories or just reaching today's end. Your experience of gratitude does not remove your hardships, yet it provides you gentler perspectives on them. The concept reminds you that although life creates disorder and unsteadiness it carries many special things to acknowledge and value.

Whenever you feel like focusing on problems, please stop yourself at that moment to observe positive aspects instead. Take a breath. Look around. You should observe both positive and negative events unfolding in your environment. Your Wi-Fi stability during an online call combined with the accomplishments of finishing a book and healthy plant growth despite your poor watering routine proves that the situation has at least one thing going in your favor.

Because let's be honest—some days, just keeping yourself fed, hydrated, and semi-functional is an achievement. And if that's the best you can do today, celebrate it. Because gratitude isn't about having a perfect life—it's about learning to love the one you have, one small, beautiful moment at a time.

Chapter 11
Overcoming Disruptions

Life is not about waiting for the storm to pass, but about learning to dance in the rain."

– Vivian Greene

Life isn't a perfectly choreographed routine—it's more like a blooper reel with occasional moments of grace. Even the most balanced body, sharpest mind, and most connected soul can stumble. Burnout sneaks in like a Netflix binge that lasts three seasons too long, negative self-talk shows up uninvited like that relative who critiques everything, and spiritual crises make you question whether you're living your purpose or just living for pizza delivery.

Disruptions are inevitable—but they're also opportunities to pause, reflect, and realign. This chapter dives into the common challenges that throw the body, mind, and soul out of sync and offers actionable strategies, along with real-life examples, to help you find your rhythm again when life feels overwhelming.

Burnout: The Body's SOS Signal

Burnout isn't just about being tired—it's like your body sending you a breakup text that says, "We need to talk." It happens when you push yourself beyond your limits, ignoring all the red flags (and probably some green smoothies).

- **Signs of Burnout:**
  - ☐ Chronic exhaustion, even after sleeping in on a Saturday.
  - ☐ Frequent illnesses that seem to say, "Rest, or I'll make you."
  - ☐ A lack of motivation—even for binge-watching your favorite show.

- **How to Overcome It:**
  - ☐ **Rest and Replenish:** Treat sleep like it's Beyoncé—make it a priority. Pair it with good food and hydration.
  - ☐ **Set Boundaries:** Say no to things like unnecessary meetings or helping your neighbor move...again.
  - ☐ **Reconnect with Joy:** Dance like nobody's watching (but maybe close the curtains first).

- **Example:** My friend Megha, a corporate manager, hit peak burnout during a major project. Late nights, skipped meals, and flu season finally gave her no choice but to stop. After some "me time" involving gardening and a strict "no work after 8 PM" rule, Megha was back to being her fabulous, plant-loving self—her roses bloomed, and so did her productivity.

Negative Self-Talk: The Mind's Saboteur

The mind is powerful—like a lawyer who's good at arguing against you. Phrases like "I'm not good enough" or "I'll never succeed" can turn even a great day into an internal roast session.

- **Signs of Negative Self-Talk:**
  - ☐ Self-criticism that makes Gordon Ramsay seem gentle.
  - ☐ Fear of failure—or worse, being caught singing in the shower.
  - ☐ Comparing yourself to others like you're the judge on a reality show no one asked for.

- **How to Overcome It:**
  - ☐ **Practice Self-Compassion:** Be your own cheerleader. Bonus points if you pom-pom.
  - ☐ **Challenge the Thoughts:** Ask, "Who wrote this script, and why are they so dramatic?"
  - ☐ **Reframe Your Perspective:** Turn "I failed" into "I'm learning." You didn't burn dinner—you just creatively caramelized it.

- **Example:** My friend Ravi landed his dream job but thought, "I don't deserve to be here." (Spoiler: He did.) Journaling his weekly wins—like "nailed that meeting" or "made coffee without spilling"—helped him see he wasn't just surviving; he was thriving.

Spiritual Crises: The Soul's Call for Connection

A spiritual crisis is like your soul saying, "Hey, remember me?" It's that existential moment when everything feels hollow, even your favorite pizza.

- **Signs of a Spiritual Crisis:**
  - ☐ Feeling lost, like when you realize you're in the wrong Zoom meeting.
  - ☐ Questioning beliefs that used to feel as solid as your Wi-Fi (before the outage).
  - ☐ Longing for deeper meaning—or at least a better horoscope.

- **How to Overcome It:**
  - ☐ **Seek Stillness:** Meditation, prayer, or just staring at the ceiling until it starts making sense.
  - ☐ **Reconnect with Nature:** Hug a tree. Or at least say hi to it.
  - ☐ **Explore New Perspectives:** Read, listen, or talk to someone wise—preferably someone who doesn't start every sentence with "Actually…"

- **Example:** After a breakup, Ananya felt adrift—like a ship without a Netflix account. She took up hiking, and the mountains didn't just give her a great view—they gave her clarity. Plus, her step count skyrocketed.

The Ripple Effect: How Disruptions Spread

Disruptions rarely stay in their lane. Burnout affects your mind, making you forget where you left your phone (it's in your hand). Negative self-talk saps the energy you need to even look for it. And a spiritual crisis can leave you staring at the fridge, wondering if snacks are the answer (they might be).

Understanding this ripple effect is key to tackling disruptions holistically. When one part falters, give the others some extra love.

Realigning the Trinity

When life feels overwhelming, here's your game plan:

1. Pause and Assess:

- ☐ Ask yourself, "Is my body crying for a nap, my mind for calm, or my soul for a cat video?"

2. Start Small:

- For example:
    - ☐ Tired? Take a water break—and maybe throw in a stretch.
    - ☐ Overwhelmed? Try 5 minutes of deep breathing (or just a deep sigh—it counts).
    - ☐ Disconnected? Write down three things that don't suck right now.

3. Lean on Support:

- ☐ Talk to someone who makes you laugh, listen, or feel seen. Bonus if they bring snacks.

4. Revisit Your Foundations:

- ☐ Reconnect with habits that make you feel human—whether it's yoga, journaling, or belting out karaoke in your car.

5. Give Yourself Grace:

  ☐ Remember, even superheroes take off their capes to do laundry.

The Humor in Overcoming Disruptions

Let's be honest: disruptions don't come with a heads-up. Burnout might hit right after you declare yourself a "productivity ninja." Negative self-talk loves popping up mid-presentation (thanks, brain). And spiritual crises? They strike when you're stuck in traffic, wondering if you took a wrong turn in life—or just on this highway.

The key is to laugh when you can. Life is messy, and so is this journey. But who said you can't find comedy gold in the chaos? Embrace the missteps, failed attempts, and unintentional karaoke sessions as part of the dance.

A Final Thought

Overcoming disruptions isn't about avoiding them or pretending they don't exist—it's about The essential practice of disruption recovery involves active acceptance that disruptions will happen naturally in human life. You should embrace life as a jazz improvisation rather than a flawless performance because it brings unanticipated musical notes alongside adaptive opportunities. The breathtaking aspect exists in personal fortitude rather than flawless execution because life continues with resilience regardless of its temporary shifts.

All disruptions represent important indicators including burnout, self-doubt and spiritual crises. These interruptions lead us to stop what we are doing so we can think about essential matters. Never resist these experiences because they serve as valuable learning opportunities to develop yourself. The path you walk forward depends on your response to missteps because you determine what follows setbacks.

Every disruption carries a lesson. Burnout forces people to learn about scheduling proper downtime along with establishing clear limits. Those negative thoughts in your mind force you to create brand new mental messages. Your search for inner meaning begins after experiencing a deep spiritual crisis that forces you to seek it. These moments of discomfort create chances for people to strengthen themselves by grounding down and increasing their self-awareness.

So, when life feels overwhelming, remember this: the music never truly stops. It might slow down or change tempo, but it's always there, waiting for you to join in again. Take the time to catch your breath, reset your footing, and re-enter the dance with renewed energy and purpose. Life is a series of rhythms, and with every disruption comes the chance to find your balance, refine your steps, and create a melody that's uniquely yours.

Keep dancing—because every stumble adds depth to your story and every recovery brings you closer to mastering the art of living with grace and joy.

Chapter 12
Creating a Personal Practice

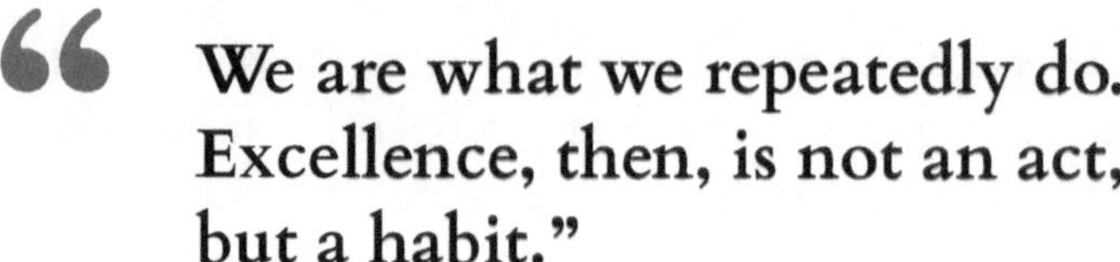

> We are what we repeatedly do.
> Excellence, then, is not an act,
> but a habit."
>
> *– Aristotle*

Life thrives on rhythms, but let's be honest creating a personal practice can sometimes feel like trying to choreograph a dance routine while juggling flaming torches. One day, you're a zen master meditating at sunrise; the next, you're scarfing down a Pop-Tart in traffic because your "morning routine" went rogue. And that's okay! The point isn't perfection—it's finding a groove that works for *you*.

A personal practice is about crafting small rituals that nurture your body, sharpen your mind, and uplift your soul. It's not a military boot camp; it's a flexible, forgiving framework that helps you show up for yourself, even when life gets messy.

Why Personal Practices Matter

Let's face it—when left to its own devices, life has a way of throwing curveballs. A well-designed personal practice helps you:

- **Find Stability in Chaos:** Think of your routine as the calm in your stormy inbox.

- **Feel More Balanced:** It's like carrying a portable Wi-Fi hotspot for your soul—always connected.

- **Show Yourself Some Love:** You deserve care, even if your laundry pile says otherwise.

Step 1: Reflect on What You Need

Before diving in, ask yourself:

- **Body:** Do you need more energy? Fewer random aches? Or just an excuse to stop doom-scrolling?

- **Mind:** Are you feeling scattered, stressed, or one YouTube rabbit hole away from losing it?

- **Soul:** Do you miss that spark of joy or purpose? Or are you just curious about why everyone keeps talking about "grounding"?

Example: My friend Sanjay realized his body was demanding stretches (his back popped like bubble wrap every morning), his mind craved quiet (bye-bye, Twitter debates), and his soul needed something more profound than Netflix marathons. Spoiler alert: Sanjay is now thriving with a 10-minute daily routine.

Step 2: Start Small (and Avoid Overwhelm)

Think of your personal practice like seasoning food—you don't dump the entire jar of salt in on Day 1. Start with bite-sized habits:

- **Body:**

  - ☐ Do two stretches while the coffee brews.

  - ☐ Take the stairs instead of the elevator.

  - ☐ Dance like no one's watching (preferably when no one actually *is* watching).

- **Mind:**

  - ☐ Spend 5 minutes journaling about anything—yes, even your annoyance at your neighbor's barking dog.

  - ☐ Do a quick mental declutter: write down your to-do list so it's not bouncing around in your head.

  - ☐ Try a guided meditation app that doesn't make you fall asleep mid-session.

- **Soul:**

  - ☐ Step outside and marvel at how the clouds look like animals (or that one time they resembled pancakes).

  - ☐ Whisper three things you're grateful for while brushing your teeth.

  - ☐ Light a candle and stare at it for a minute. Bonus points if you don't accidentally start thinking about work.

Example: My friend Riya started her soul practice by spending 2 minutes a day staring at the sky. It felt silly at first, but now she swears it's her favorite mini escape from the chaos of office emails.

Step 3: Build a Routine That Works for You

You don't have to wake up at 4 a.m. or meditate on a mountain to craft a great practice. (Unless you're into that—then by all means, go full monk mode.) The best routines fit seamlessly into your life:

- **Morning Ritual:**
  Start your day with purpose:

  - ☐ Stretch, breathe, or do 10 jumping jacks (if your neighbors don't mind the thumping).

  - ☐ Read a page of something inspiring, like a book or your own witty tweets.

  - ☐ Whisper a mantra, like "I've got this" or "Coffee first, universe later."

- **Midday Reset:**
  Give yourself a midday pick-me-up:

  - ☐ Walk around your office/house/neighborhood.

  - ☐ Do a two-minute gratitude check-in: "I'm thankful I didn't spill lunch on my shirt today."

  - ☐ Listen to a favorite song and dance like a dork in your living room.

- **Evening Wind-Down:**
  Close the day on a peaceful note:

  - ☐ Journal about one win of the day (even if it's "I remembered to drink water").

  - ☐ Meditate or pray—whatever feels right.

  - ☐ Read a book...or at least the back of the cereal box if that's all you've got energy for.

Example: My friend Vikram crafted a routine of morning yoga, a midday walk, and an evening gratitude ritual. Except for the days he accidentally binge-watches cricket instead. Balance, right?

Step 4: Stay Flexible and Laugh at the Chaos

Your practice should feel like a friend, not a drill sergeant. Some days, life will derail your plans, and that's okay:

- **Be Kind to Yourself:** Missed your morning meditation? Do a 60-second-deep breath before bed instead.

- **Infuse Fun:** Play around with your rituals. Try dancing to 80s music, journaling with colorful pens, or walking in the rain (umbrella optional).

Example: Journaling turned out to be something Pooja strongly disliked. She created voice notes to share her daily activities including her humorous side. Voice notes message has become her favorite routine as she has built up a collection of brief motivational messages.

Step 5: Reflect and Adjust

A personal practice evolves just like you do. Every month or so, pause and ask yourself:

- **Body Check:** Am I feeling stronger, or is my energy still on "low battery"?

- **Mind Check:** Am I thinking clearer, or do I still feel like a hamster on a wheel?

- **Soul Check:** Am I more connected, or does everything still feel… meh?

Example: Sanjay realized his morning yoga wasn't cutting it anymore, so he swapped it for an outdoor jog. Now, he swears by the combo of running and nature to clear his head.

The Humor in Personal Practices

Here's the truth: Personal practices rarely go as planned. You'll wake up late and skip your morning stretch. You'll meditate for 5 seconds before a rogue mosquito attacks. Or you'll start a gratitude journal only to realize half your entries are about coffee.

But that's the beauty of it! Your practice doesn't have to be perfect—it just has to be yours. The more you laugh at the mishaps, the easier it is to stay consistent.

A Final Thought: Your Practice, Your Power

Your personal practice beyond being a set of daily routines functions as an honorable representation of self-importance and serves as both a wellness pledge and peaceful defiance against everyday disruptions. The key aspect of a personal practice does not depend on rigid scheduling or absolute adherence to early morning routines simply because an internet figure claims so. A natural sustainable and fulfilling rhythm is what you should aim to establish in your life.

A personal practice develops consistently with the person who practices it. The experience that succeeds today could transform after one month which remains acceptable. When your daily activities unfold naturally, they become like practicing an already familiar tune. One day your practice flows smoothly but, on another day, it seems uncoordinated while you practice new steps to the song. Continuing to arrive at your practice while changing it along with your growth together with self-compassion will lead to improvement.

Instead of chasing a flawless routine, embrace the **real-life version**—the one that includes good days, messy days, and everything in between. Some days, you'll complete your full morning ritual, feel zen, and sip tea while journaling about life's beauty. Other days, your "practice" might just be remembering to drink water and not lose your patience in traffic. **Both counts.**

Your personal practice isn't about checking boxes; it's about building a relationship with yourself. It's a moment each day where you pause, breathe, and remind yourself that **you matter.** It's a way to stay anchored when life gets overwhelming, a way to bring joy into the ordinary, and a way to ensure that no matter how busy, chaotic, or unpredictable things get—you always have something to return to.

So go ahead—experiment, tweak, and refine your practice. If something doesn't work, change it. If life gets in the way, adapt. The only rule is to **keep going.** Because at the end of the day, it's not about having the perfect routine—it's about having one that makes you feel more **you.**

And that? That's the real magic.

Part 4

LIVING THE TRINITY

Chapter 13

The Balanced Life in Relationships

> **A healthy relationship is built on unwavering balance—giving and receiving, speaking and listening, understanding and being understood."**
>
> – *Doe Zantamata*

Picture this: You've had a stressful day, and your mind is frazzled. You walk into the kitchen, see your partner staring at their phone, and immediately think, *"Why aren't they helping me?!"* What you don't realize is they're Googling "quick ways to make someone smile after a tough day." Boom. Cue unnecessary drama.

This, my friend, is where inner harmony saves the day. When your body, mind, and soul are balanced, you approach relationships with a calm, open perspective instead of being a live wire ready to spark at the tiniest misstep. Let's break it down.

Inner Harmony = Outer Connection

When you're balanced internally, it creates a ripple effect on your relationships:

1. **Body:** You have the energy and patience to engage meaningfully with others. It's easier to be present at dinner with your family when you're not running on caffeine fumes and two hours of sleep.

2. **Mind:** Mental clarity helps you communicate effectively, avoiding those "Wait, that's not what I meant!" moments.

3. **Soul:** A fulfilled soul allows you to connect on a deeper level, whether it's sharing dreams with your partner or giggling over old stories with friends.

The Miscommunication Tango

Here's a classic example:

I once asked a friend to "pick up some snacks" for a movie night. In my mind, I was envisioning chips, popcorn, and maybe some chocolate. My friend, however, showed up with...baby carrots and hummus. *Carrots.* For *movie night.* Was I annoyed? Sure. But instead of snapping, I took a deep breath (thank you, balanced mind!) and calmly asked, "Was this your idea of a plot twist?" We laughed it off, and the next time, I brought the snacks myself.

The takeaway? Inner balance gives you the tools to handle missteps with humor instead of hostility.

How Inner Balance Improves Relationships

1. **Partnerships**
When you're grounded, you're less likely to take things personally. If your partner forgets to

unload the dishwasher, instead of assuming they're plotting your demise, you realize they might just be distracted. Harmony helps you approach situations with curiosity rather than conflict.

Funny Scenario:
My friend Sarah once told me she got into an argument with her husband because he didn't respond to her text asking what he wanted for dinner. Turns out, he was chopping onions for the *exact same dinner* she was planning. Lesson learned: balance helps you laugh instead of launching into battle.

2. **Family**
Families are often where we're most reactive (*because* we're so close). Inner harmony helps you respond thoughtfully rather than reacting emotionally. It's the difference between calmly explaining why you don't want another slice of your aunt's infamous "mystery casserole" and blurting, "No thanks, I'd rather eat a shoe."

Example:
One holiday, my cousin accidentally took my coat home. Instead of freaking out, I texted her, "I see you liked my coat so much you decided to adopt it. Can I visit it tomorrow?" She laughed and brought it back with cookies as an apology.

3. **Friendships**
Balanced friendships thrive on mutual support. When you're at peace with yourself, you can truly

celebrate your friend's successes without envy—
and show up for them when they're struggling.

Real-Life Moment:
A friend called me in tears after a rough day. I was
tired, but my balanced self said, "This isn't about
you—be there for her." We ended up laughing at
ridiculous things by the end of the call, and she
texted later, "You saved my sanity tonight."

Practical Tips for Harmonious Relationships

1. **Pause Before Reacting**
   When you feel triggered, take a breath and ask,
   "Am I responding from balance or burnout?"

   Humorous Tip:
   Before snapping, picture yourself as a sitcom
   character. Would the audience laugh at your
   overreaction? If yes, dial it down.

2. **Communicate Clearly**
   Balanced minds mean better communication. Say
   what you mean, and clarify what you hear.

   Example:
   Friend: "I'm fine."
   You (calmly): "Okay, but are you *fine* or 'I'm
   pretending to be fine' fine?" (Spoiler: It's always
   the latter.)

3. **Practice Gratitude**
   Notice and appreciate the good in your
   relationships. Thank your partner for making
   coffee or your mom for sending you memes.

Funny Perspective:
Gratitude includes celebrating small wins, like your roommate finally replacing the toilet paper roll *without* you asking.

4. **Set Boundaries**
Balance means knowing your limits. It's okay to say no to a party if your soul is screaming, *"Netflix and pajamas!"*

The Humor in Relationship Balance

Let's be honest: balancing relationships isn't all deep conversations and magical moments. Sometimes, it's messy and ridiculous. Like the time my partner insisted we could "build IKEA furniture together without arguing." Spoiler: we couldn't. But instead of dwelling on the chaos, we ended up laughing at how the instructions looked like they were drawn by an alien.

Relationships thrive not because we're perfect, but because we're willing to laugh at the imperfections—and keep trying anyway.

Final Thought: Your Inner World Shapes Your Outer World

When you're balanced within yourself, you create a safe, supportive space for the people around you. Relationships aren't about being flawless; they're about showing up, being honest, and finding humor in the hiccups.

At the heart of every relationship—whether romantic, familial, or platonic—is the energy you bring to it. If your inner world is chaotic, it's easy to project that turmoil onto others. But when you cultivate balance within yourself, you naturally create a space of calm, understanding, and connection for the people around you.

Think of yourself as a tuning fork: when you're in harmony, your relationships resonate with that same energy. Instead of reacting from stress, you respond with patience. Instead of assuming the worst, you approach situations with curiosity. Instead of letting small annoyances turn into full-blown arguments, you find humor in the hiccups.

So, next time life hands you a relationship challenge, remember pause, breathe, and maybe crack a joke. Because sometimes, the best way to handle miscommunication is to say, *"Okay, but seriously, who brings carrots to movie night?"* And then laugh about it together.

Chapter 14

The Trinity and Gratitude in the World

> **"** Gratitude turns what we have into enough, and more. It turns denial into acceptance, chaos into order, confusion into clarity... It makes sense of our past, brings peace for today, and creates a vision for tomorrow."

> *– Melody Beattie*

Imagine this: You're running late, juggling coffee, your laptop bag, and existential dread about an upcoming meeting. A stranger holds the elevator for you, and suddenly your day feels a little brighter. You mumble a grateful "thank you," and guess what? That simple act of acknowledgment might inspire them to pay it forward—maybe they'll help someone else later in the day, creating a ripple effect of goodness.

Gratitude isn't just about journaling three things you're thankful for (although that's fantastic). It's a force that can extend outward, positively shaping careers, communities, and even global connections. When balanced within the trinity of body, mind, and soul, gratitude becomes a superpower that not only grounds us but also lifts the world around us.

How Gratitude Ripples Outward

1. **In Careers: The Gratitude Advantage**
   Gratitude in the workplace goes beyond polite emails that end with "Thank you for your time." When you genuinely express appreciation to your colleagues, it fosters collaboration and trust. And when you're balanced within yourself, showing gratitude becomes second nature instead of feeling like a forced corporate exercise.

   Example:
   A friend of mine once baked cookies for her team after a tough project. (Yes, cookies!) She didn't just thank them—she handed out chocolate chip appreciation. Not only did it boost morale, but months later, when she needed help on another project, her team was all in. Turns out, gratitude is the secret ingredient to more than just cookies.

2. **In Communities: The Multiplier Effect**
   Gratitude within communities creates a culture of kindness. When you thank the barista, compliment your neighbor's garden, or join a local cleanup drive, you're not just expressing gratitude—you're sparking it in others. Balanced individuals who are grounded in mind, body, and soul are more likely to engage in these acts of kindness, knowing that they're contributing to something greater.

Funny Moment:
A neighborhood group near me started a "thank your delivery person" initiative during the holidays. One family left cookies and a note on their porch. Their delivery guy? He responded with a drawing of a cartoon smiley face on their next package. Gratitude brings out creativity—and apparently, hidden artistic talents.

3. **Globally: The Big Picture of Gratitude**
Gratitude has no borders. Supporting a global cause, donating to charities, or even sharing a kind comment online can create waves you may never see. A grateful soul realizes that every act—no matter how small—has an impact.

Real-Life Example:
Remember those viral videos of strangers helping strangers? Like a commuter pushing a stuck car in a rainstorm or someone paying for a line of strangers' coffee? Gratitude inspires action, and action inspires connection, whether it's in your town or halfway across the world.

Practical Ways to Extend Gratitude to the World

1. **Volunteer Your Time**
Nothing says "I care" like showing up for your community. Whether it's tutoring kids, planting trees, or spending time at a shelter, your actions can inspire others to do the same.

Humorous Spin:
One of my friends volunteered at a community garden. She didn't realize how bad she was at gardening until someone kindly said, "We'll handle the plants—can you hold the hose?" Her takeaway? Gratitude is about effort, not perfection.

2. **Be Generous with Compliments**
    Gratitude isn't just about saying "thank you"; it's about recognizing and acknowledging others. Compliment a colleague's creativity or your favorite local restaurant's amazing food.

    Example:
    A guy at my gym once complimented an older man on his push-up form. The older guy looked genuinely touched and said, "That's the nicest thing anyone's said to me this week." Cue smiles all around.

3. **Donate What You Can**
    Whether it's money, clothes, or books, giving from a place of abundance (even if it's small) makes a difference. Gratitude grows when you realize how much you have to give.

    Fun Anecdote:
    A friend donated a few old coats to a charity drive. A week later, she saw someone wearing one of her coats on the street. She ran up to say hello, and the person jokingly said, "Nice coat, right?" Gratitude, shared, creates memorable moments.

4. **Pay It Forward**

    The simplest acts can have the greatest impact. Buy someone's coffee, leave an encouraging note for a stranger, or let someone cut ahead of you in traffic (if you're feeling saintly).

    Humorous Scenario:

    I once paid for the person behind me at a toll booth. They honked and waved furiously, and for a second, I thought I'd done something wrong. Turns out, they were just excited to thank me.

Balancing Gratitude with the Trinity

- **Body:** A healthy body allows you to show up for others physically, whether it's volunteering or helping a friend move that ridiculously heavy couch.

- **Mind:** A clear mind helps you see opportunities to express gratitude, rather than being consumed by stress or negativity.

- **Soul:** A fulfilled soul recognizes the beauty in small moments, like the laugh of a child or the kindness of a stranger.

Gratitude flows most freely when all three are in sync.

The Humor in Global Gratitude

Let's face it: gratitude isn't always glamorous. Sometimes, it's awkward. Like when you try to thank someone and accidentally blurt out, "You too!" (Yes, I've said "You too" to a waiter wishing me a great meal.) Or when you send a thank-you email and forget to attach the thing you're thanking them for asking about.

The beauty of gratitude, though, is that it doesn't need to be perfect. It just needs to be real.

Final Thought: The World Runs on Gratitude

Think of gratitude as the world's invisible fuel. It powers connections, strengthens communities, and bridges divides. When you approach life with a balanced trinity and an attitude of gratitude, you become part of something bigger—something that ripples outward, touching lives in ways you may never see but can always feel.

The practice of gratitude perpetually endures because it reverberates among people. Any instance of gratitude creates an endless chain reaction of thankfulness for others. Today's kindness can create a response that can come back to you from an unexpected person many years later. The power of gratitude extends across all time periods as well as geographic locations without requiring personal relationships. You illuminate the present by making a choice for gratitude which generates an endless chain of positive effects that no one knows how far it will reach.

Therefore, begin expressing gratitude toward your barista while feeling free to offer a friendly word about your neighbor's garish light display or donate that faded jacket which doesn't serve you. Who knows? Your actions can spark a universal wave of kindness that begins with each laughter and each compliment coupled with each cookie you share.

Chapter 15

The Trinity at Work: Bringing Balance to the 9-to-5 (and beyond)

> **You will never feel truly satisfied by work until you are satisfied by life."**
>
> *– Heather Schuck*

Work can often feel like a circus, where you're not just juggling tasks but also trying to ride a unicycle while taming a lion of deadlines. Balancing the trinity—body, mind, and soul—might sound like a lofty ideal in a professional setting, but it's not just possible; it's transformative. By maintaining harmony within yourself, you can create a work life that's productive, purposeful, and—dare I say it—enjoyable.

Let's explore how you can incorporate balance into your workday and see how it can turn those endless Zoom calls into opportunities for growth and fulfillment.

How to Balance the Trinity at Work

1. **The Body at Work: Move, Nourish, and Rest**

   Your body might be the least glamorous part of the trinity to think about at work, but it's the foundation. A well-cared-for body supports mental clarity and soulful engagement.

- ☐ **Take Mini Breaks:** Don't wait for burnout to remind you that you're human. A quick stretch, a brisk walk around the office, or even standing up while taking a call can do wonders.

- ☐ **Snack Smartly:** Trade the vending machine candy bar for a handful of nuts or fruit. Think of it as fuel for your brain, not just a sugar rush to survive the afternoon slump.

- ☐ **Rest Your Eyes:** If you're glued to a screen all day, the 20-20-20 rule is your friend. Every 20 minutes, look at something 20 feet away for 20 seconds. Your future, non-strained eyes will thank you.

Example:

A colleague of mine, Raj, used to power through his lunch breaks like a warrior, shoveling in food while staring at spreadsheets. One day, he decided to eat outside under a tree instead. Not only did his digestion thank him, but he also returned to his desk with ideas so good, even his boss called him a genius. Sometimes, fresh air and mindful chewing are all you need to unlock brilliance.

2. **The Mind at Work: Focus, Flex, and Breathe**

Your mind is the engine driving your professional life, but engines need maintenance. Overworking leads to stress, which clouds judgment and creativity.

☐ **Prioritize Tasks:** Start your day by listing three top priorities. Focus on those first, and let the smaller tasks fall in line.

☐ **Take Mental Breaks:** Schedule short moments to zone out or meditate. (Yes, even two minutes of breathing deeply at your desk counts!)

☐ **Practice Emotional Intelligence:** Respond to challenging emails or meetings with a cool head. Take a moment to reflect before you react—this is where mindfulness comes in handy.

Funny Moment:

My friend, Sara, once responded to a client's unreasonable demand with, "Sure, I'll send that report over yesterday." When the client didn't catch the sarcasm, Sara realized she needed to meditate before typing emails. Now, she starts every morning with five minutes of mindful breathing—and her emails are both calmer and typo-free.

3. **The Soul at Work: Find Purpose, Spread Joy, and Connect**

Here's where the magic happens. Soulful engagement at work is about finding meaning in what you do and building connections that go beyond to-do lists.

☐ **Find Your "Why":** Remind yourself why you do what you do. Maybe it's supporting your family, building a legacy, or simply learning and growing each day.

☐ **Celebrate Small Wins:** Whether it's completing a project or surviving a tough meeting, take a moment to acknowledge your efforts. Gratitude feeds the soul.

☐ **Build Relationships:** Be the person who remembers birthdays, asks about weekend plans, and shares a laugh during coffee breaks. Relationships make work feel less like work.

Example:

In my previous job, a colleague named Ananya had this magical ability to brighten everyone's day. She once organized a surprise "Tea and Trivia" break during a particularly stressful quarter. It didn't fix all our problems, but it reminded us that we're human—and it gave the soul a reason to smile in the middle of chaos.

Real-Life Stories of Trinity Balance at Work

1. **Balancing Focus with Breaks:**

   Rohit, a software developer, struggled with staying focused during long coding sessions. He started following the Pomodoro technique (working in 25-minute bursts with 5-minute breaks). During those breaks, he would stretch or take a few mindful breaths. Not only did his productivity skyrocket, but he also started enjoying his work again.

2. **Finding Soulful Purpose in Daily Tasks:**

   Maya, a teacher, dreaded grading papers. Then, she started attaching a short note of encouragement to each student's assignment. What began as a small act of kindness turned into a soulful practice that reminded her why she loved teaching in the first place. Her students? They started turning in better work, inspired by her feedback.

3. **Prioritizing Health at Work:**

   Arjun, a sales manager, would often skip meals to meet targets. After a near-burnout moment, he set a timer to eat lunch and drink water regularly. By taking care of his body, he found he had more energy to close deals—and fewer post-lunch sugar crashes.

Humor in the Workplace Trinity

Balancing the trinity at work isn't all zen and rainbows. It's also about laughing at the chaos:

- When your "quick stretch" turns into an accidental downward dog in the middle of a meeting.

- When you try mindfulness but fall asleep mid-meditation at your desk.

- When you "celebrate small wins" by eating a whole pizza after sending a single email.

Work-life balance is a journey, not a destination, so don't take it too seriously.

Final Thought: Balance as the Ultimate Productivity Hack

When your body feels strong, your mind stays sharp, and your soul finds joy, work stops feeling like an endless to-do list and transforms into something more meaningful. It becomes a space where you're not just completing tasks but growing, learning, and making a real impact. Instead of feeling drained at the end of the day, you begin to find energy in the rhythm of balance—fueling your body with the right nourishment, giving your mind the clarity it needs to focus, and allowing your soul to find fulfillment in even the smallest moments.

The practice of balance in work life does not require perfect outcomes or strict scheduling methods. Self-awareness provides direction for how you should proceed since it helps you understand both work moments and rest periods. You should transform the current attitude of tolerating work into viewing it as a platform enabling your individual development and professional progression. When you allow yourself and others room for mindful interaction alongside personal movement you develop a workplace where productivity manifests naturally instead of always being pursued.

When life needs refreshment walk outdoors while sending appreciative emails to others as well as recognizing minor achievements because positive moments compound into meaningful accomplishments. Your approach to work balance will show you work is about thriving instead of just surviving from day to day. Productivity develops into a self-generated result from maintaining a balanced lifestyle.

Chapter 16

The Infinite Journey: Balance as a Lifelong Adventure

> **Balance is not something you find; it's something you create."**
>
> – *Jana Kingsford*

Balance is not a destination marked with a shiny trophy or a perfectly serene Instagram photo of you meditating at sunrise with avocado toast by your side. It's more like a rollercoaster—a constant series of ups and downs, twists and turns, and moments where you scream, "Why did I sign up for this?"

To achieve balance, you should not focus on perfection but on constant development. Life requires learning how to dance between chaos together with facing missteps and discovering calmness amidst turbulent times. Balance transforms as human beings develop over time. This quality creates its beautiful essence.

Let's reflect on what it means to embrace this infinite journey, imperfections and all.

1. Balance Is Fluid, Not Fixed

Life changes. Some days, you feel like a Zen master who has everything under control. Other days, you're eating cereal for dinner at 11 PM while wondering how your laundry pile turned into a small mountain. That's okay! Balance shifts based on your circumstances, and that's completely normal.

Key Insight:
Balance isn't about achieving a perfect 33.3% split between body, mind, and soul every day. It's about responding to what you need most in the moment. Maybe today, your soul needs a walk in the park, but tomorrow, your body might demand a full night's sleep.

Funny Example:
Take my friend Arjun, who once planned the ultimate "balanced day." Morning yoga? Check. Healthy smoothie for breakfast? Double check. Mindful journaling session? Nailed it. By lunchtime, he was so deep into his newfound Zen that he forgot to pack a lunch for work. By 2 PM, his stomach was growling so loudly that his colleagues thought there was construction happening outside. He ended his "perfectly balanced day" with a vending machine feast of chips and a Coke.

2. Embrace the Imperfections

Perfection is overrated—and let's be honest, it's boring. What makes life interesting are the quirks, the missteps, and the funny stories you tell later. Balance isn't about getting it right all the time; it's about showing up and trying, even when things go hilariously wrong.

Key Insight:
When you embrace imperfections, you give yourself permission to grow. Every misstep is a lesson, and every lesson brings you closer to the version of yourself you want to be.

Humor Alert:
I once tried to balance work, fitness, and mindfulness by multitasking—walking on a treadmill while listening to a mindfulness podcast. The result? I was so focused on the podcast's "be aware of your breath" advice that I completely missed the part about being aware of where my feet were. One trip and a very dramatic fall later, I had a sore knee, a broken ego, and a story that's still making my friends laugh.

3. Celebrate Progress, Not Perfection

Progress deserves a round of applause, no matter how small. Did you drink an extra glass of water today? Did you step outside for five minutes of fresh air? Did you manage to meditate for three minutes before your mind wandered to your to-do list? Celebrate it all!

Key Insight:
Progress builds momentum. The more you acknowledge your wins, the more motivated you'll feel to keep going. Over time, these small steps add up to big changes.

Funny Example:
A friend of mine, Priya, decided to start journaling every day as part of her "balanced life" plan. On day one, she wrote a heartfelt entry about her goals and dreams. By day three, her entry read, "Ate pizza. Feeling full. Too tired to

write. Goodnight." But guess what? She kept going, and by the end of the month, she'd built a journaling habit—even if some entries were just about pizza.

4. The Journey Is the Destination

If you're waiting for a day when everything feels perfectly balanced, spoiler alert: it's probably not coming. And that's okay! The magic lies in the journey itself—in the messy, joyful, unpredictable process of figuring it all out.

Key Insight:
When you stop chasing the idea of "perfect balance" and start appreciating the process, life becomes a lot more enjoyable. Every day is an opportunity to learn, grow, and try again.

Humor Alert:
Remember that time I committed to meditating for 10 minutes every morning? By day five, my "meditation" turned into me sitting cross-legged, making a grocery list in my head. Was it perfect? Nope. Did it help me avoid forgetting milk that week? Absolutely.

Humor in Life's Journey of Balance

Let's be honest trying to maintain balance in life can sometimes feel like a sitcom where you're both the main character and the clumsy sidekick. No matter how much you plan, life has a way of throwing unexpected plot twists your way.

Ever tried waking up early for a mindful morning routine, only to snooze your alarm five times and wake up in a panic? Or promised yourself a "balanced diet," then proceeded to eat an entire tub of ice cream because, well, life happens? Balance is not about getting it right every single time—it's about rolling with the punches and laughing at the moments where things go hilariously wrong.

One time, I signed up for a meditation retreat to find inner peace. Within the first hour, my mind had wandered from deep breathing to wondering if I had locked my front door, debating what to eat for dinner, and mentally redoing my entire budget for the month. By the time the session ended, I had found zero enlightenment but had successfully planned my grocery list. Life's balance is a mix of effort and embracing our human quirks.

The secret to achieve balance includes recognizing errors will happen and an ability to use humor which acts as a great motivator. A person who never laughs at their own mistakes while attempting goals certainly needs to reconsider their existence.

Final Thought: The Art of Balancing Without Breaking

We dedicate our lives to achieving balance because the perfect state of equilibrium can't be achieved permanently. The process of achieving balance teaches individuals to adjust their approach according to the changes that occur in life.

The perfect combination of sharp mind and energized body and peaceful soul will only occur occasionally throughout your journey. Your daily life may include shedding coffee on your favorite shirt while forgetting essential obligations without knowing where the instruction booklet for being an adult is hidden. The process includes these two conditions as equal elements toward becoming impartial.

Finding contentment comes from discovering happiness in unpredictable situations. Your ability to manage life involves proper timing of your actions between driving ahead and pressing pause between seeking order and forgiving yourself for mistakes. The path to advancement stands as the only realistic target instead of achieving flawless excellence.

Life stays unpredictable and we should acknowledge it. Savor each accomplishment but gather knowledge from any mistakes you make as your main goal should be to savor this journey. True balance emerges from navigating the life's evolving rhythms using your grin and enjoying cookies occasionally.

Part 5

EMBRACING SELF-COMPASSION

Chapter 17

The Power of Self-Kindness: The Art of Being Your Own Best Friend

> **Talk to yourself like you would to someone you love."**
>
> *– Brené Brown*

When was the last time you gave yourself a compliment, a break, or even a pat on the back? If your answer is "Umm, never?" you're not alone. Most of us are harder on ourselves than we are on anyone else. We'd comfort a friend with kind words if they made a mistake, but when it comes to ourselves, we become drill sergeants with no chill.

Self-kindness isn't about being indulgent or lazy; it's about acknowledging that you're human, not a robot running on deadlines and unrealistic expectations. It's about treating yourself with the same compassion you'd offer to someone you care about. Let's explore why self-kindness is a superpower you need in your life—and yes, we'll sprinkle in some humor and real-life examples along the way.

1. The Case for Self-Kindness

Life can feel like a constant race, and the pressure to be perfect at everything can weigh heavily. When we don't meet these impossible standards, self-criticism kicks in. But here's the thing: beating yourself up doesn't make you better. It just makes you tired.

Key Insight:
Self-kindness acts as a buffer against the negative effects of perfectionism, guilt, and self-criticism. It allows you to fail, learn, and move forward without carrying the emotional baggage of self-loathing.

Funny Example:
Take my friend Ananya, who baked cookies for a work potluck. She accidentally used salt instead of sugar—classic mix-up. When the first brave soul bit into one, their expression screamed, "Why is this cookie so angry at me?" Ananya's initial reaction? Total meltdown. She kept saying, "I've ruined everything!" But after a few deep breaths (and a good laugh with her coworkers), she reminded herself that everyone makes mistakes. By the end of the potluck, the salty cookies had become a running joke, and Ananya had bounced back with grace—and a promise to label her containers better.

2. The Science of Self-Compassion

Research indicates that having self-compassion produces resilient outcomes in people. Research indicates that practicing self-compassion helps people fight depression and anxiety while raising their drive and general health. Bringing self-kindness into practice enables your brain to realign its response from setback reactivity to focus on personal development.

Key Insight:

Through self-kindness your mind generates an open space which enables you to work through feelings and make failures productive and continue forward. Being your own cheerleader functions better than being your own worst critic.

Humor Alert:

Your inner critic appears as a cranky feline companion who scrutinizes each of your actions from your shoulder. Being self-kind like offering warm blankets with catnip to a displeased cat produces negativity relief which paves the way for support.

3. Self-Kindness in Action

It's one thing to understand self-kindness in theory, but how do you practice it? Here are a few actionable tips to get started:

- **Talk to Yourself Like a Friend:** Would you call your best friend "an epic failure" because they forgot to reply to an email? No? Then why say it to yourself? Replace harsh self-talk with kind, understanding words.

- **Give Yourself Permission to Rest:** You don't have to earn rest by being productive 24/7. Sometimes, the kindest thing you can do is take a nap or binge-watch your favorite show guilt-free.

- **Celebrate Small Wins:** Did you wake up on time today? High five! Did you make it through a stressful meeting without losing your cool? Double high five!

Funny Example:
My friend Ravi tried to practice self-kindness by taking a mental health day. He planned a relaxing day of reading, meditating, and cooking. Instead, he accidentally spent eight hours assembling a piece of IKEA furniture and ended up with extra screws and a slightly crooked bookshelf. Instead of berating himself, Ravi decided to call it a "character-building exercise" and ordered pizza.

4. Turning Self-Kindness into a Habit

Self-kindness, like any habit, takes practice. Start small—maybe by saying one nice thing to yourself each day or forgiving yourself for one slip-up. Over time, it will become second nature, and you'll start to notice how much lighter and more positive life feels.

Key Insight:
Self-kindness isn't a one-time thing; it's a daily practice. The more you do it, the more you'll build emotional resilience and confidence.

Humor Alert:
Think of self-kindness like flossing—it feels awkward at first, but once you get into the habit, you'll wonder how you ever lived without it. And hey, if you forget a day? Be kind to yourself about that, too.

5. The Ripple Effect of Self-Kindness

When you are kind to yourself, it not only benefits you but also everyone around you. A more compassionate you are a more understanding friend, partner, and coworker. Plus, self-kindness is contagious—when others see you practicing it, they're more likely to do the same.

Funny Example:
After learning to be kinder to herself, my friend Priya started inspiring her team at work. One day, her colleague spilled coffee all over an important report. Instead of freaking out, Priya handed them a napkin and said, "Let's call this an opportunity to improve the design with some creative coffee stains."

The Humor in Self-Kindness

Let's be real: self-kindness can get messy, and that's okay. Like the time I told myself, "I'll be kind to me today and treat myself to a fancy homemade meal." Twenty minutes later, I was sitting in front of a slightly burnt grilled cheese sandwich, thinking, *Well, it's the thought that counts.*

Or when you decide to practice self-love by taking a bubble bath, only to realize you don't own a bathtub—just a shower with questionable water pressure. The beauty of self-kindness isn't in the perfection; it's in the effort. Even the awkward, slightly ridiculous moments are steps in the right direction.

Final Thought: Self-Kindness is the Foundation

The foundation for living a contented life with balance rests in self-kindness. To achieve self-kindness, it does not mean we must be flawless in every way; we should learn to defend and support ourselves throughout all situations. Your self-treatment methods determine all aspects of your existence including personal assurance levels and relationship quality as well as your capability to handle life's hurdles. Practicing self-kindness creates an internal refuge which protects your right to exist as human while letting you learn from errors without facing critical self-perception.

When supporting a friend through tough times you encourage them with positive remarks and point out their abilities before guiding them to see the overall situation. You should supply the same compassionate attitude toward yourself which you bestow upon others. The outcome would produce both a content and peaceful you and simultaneously generate a thriving version of yourself. The practice of being kind to yourself enables you to build up mental and emotional resilience for handling life's challenges gracefully and in a strong manner.

Self-kindness practices spread beneficial effects outside the person who practices them. Self-compassion with patience brings forth a natural extension of your caring behavior toward others. When you practice self-kindness, you develop the ability to see perfection in moments of imperfection within yourself as well as others.

Though self-kindness varies between moments it never must match the standards of deep meditations alongside perfect self-care routines. You may choose to buy takeout when you need rest from preparing food. When you practice self-kindness, it may involve letting out laughter at your own faults whereas before you used to let these mistakes drag you down. Self-kindness operates through flexibility since its essence appears in everyday moments that involve choosing compassion over self-judgment.

So, celebrate your efforts, no matter how small. Acknowledge your wins, even if they seem insignificant. You should show yourself compassion even when times become difficult. Above all, continue moving forward. Life includes more than achieving ideal equilibrium because it requires your complete self-acceptance of both strengths and weaknesses along with your special qualities. Excellent life fulfillment starts with becoming the companion you need the most.

Chapter 18

Forgiving Yourself:
Letting Go of Guilt

> **Forgive yourself for not knowing what you didn't know before you learned it."**
>
> – *Maya Angelou*

Self-forgiveness is one of the hardest—and most liberating—skills to master. Let's face it: we're often our own worst critics. While we'd happily reassure a friend that "everyone makes mistakes," we don't extend the same kindness to ourselves. Instead, we cling to guilt and self-judgment like an old mixtape of embarrassing songs we just can't throw away. But guilt isn't a badge of honor; it's a backpack full of rocks that keeps us stuck. Forgiving yourself isn't about erasing the past—it's about lightening the load so you can move forward.

The Burden of Guilt and Judgment

Everyone has experienced the heavy weight of guilt through a sinking emotional state. The first small pain then rapidly transforms into an expanded internal monologue which asks, "Why did I perform this action?" I should've known better. What's wrong with me?" Soon after the event you begin endlessly reliving it in your mind as though your life became a Groundhog Day sequel.

Guilt together with self-criticism creates an unbalanced state because they force us to remain mentally tied to past events. Guilt along with self-judgment drain our energy and fog our thinking power while eliminating any space for joy or advancement in life. When you have guilt on your hands you remain unable to reach future opportunities.

Reframing Mistakes as Learning Opportunities

Mistakes don't define you—they refine you. Every stumble, misstep, or facepalm-worthy moment is just a step on the ladder of growth. Instead of seeing mistakes as failures, try reframing them as opportunities to learn and improve.

Imagine you're assembling furniture from IKEA without reading the instructions (because, of course, you thought you could figure it out). Two hours in, you realize the bookshelf is upside-down. Instead of berating yourself, you laugh, fix it, and chalk it up to a lesson in humility—and the importance of diagrams.

Mistakes are the world's most underrated teachers. They help you discover what doesn't work so you can get closer to what does.

Example: A Calendar Mishap

Let's talk about my friend Raj, the king of calendar mix-ups. Raj once marked his niece's birthday party as "2 PM on Sunday." Unfortunately, the party was actually at 2 PM on *Saturday*. He showed up a day late with balloons, a heartfelt card, and a guilty look that screamed, "I'm the worst uncle ever."

But instead of wallowing in shame, Raj owned up to the mistake, made a joke about being "fashionably late by 24 hours," and took his niece out for ice cream to make up for it. By letting go of guilt, he turned an embarrassing moment into a sweet memory—and a reminder to double-check his Google Calendar.

Steps to Self-Forgiveness

1. **Acknowledge the Guilt:**
    The first step is admitting you feel guilty. Ignoring it won't make it go away (trust me, guilt is stubborn). Say it out loud or write it down: "I feel bad about [insert mistake here]."

2. **Ask Yourself: What Can I Learn?**
    Every mistake has an educational wisdom to learn from it. Your mistake offers valuable insights regarding the skills you need to master or the habits you must modify together with the knowledge that you are not limited to robotic functionality.

3. **Practice Self-Compassion:**
    Treat yourself like you'd treat a friend. Would you call your best friend a failure for accidentally replying "All" to an email chain? No. So why do it to yourself?

4. **Let It Go:**
    Picture your guilt as a balloon. Now let it float away. (If visualization is distracting, try writing

your guilt down and tearing it up—it's surprisingly cathartic!)

5. **Move Forward with Grace:**
    The past is a lesson, not a life sentence. Use the lessons you have learned while moving ahead with self-assurance and gentleness towards yourself.

The Humor in Self-Forgiveness

Self-forgiveness comes with a side of comedy. After all, the mistakes we agonize over often become the stories we laugh about later. Like the time you confidently walked into the wrong meeting and stayed for 15 minutes before realizing your mistake. Or the moment you congratulated someone on a promotion they hadn't received yet (oops).

Life is full of these little hiccups, and they're what make us human. Forgiving yourself means embracing the humor in your imperfections and moving on with a smile—even if it's a sheepish one.

Final Thought: Be Your Own Biggest Supporter

Self-forgiveness does not involve deleting mistakes or suppressing their past occurrence. The way to progress is by changing your angle so you see mistakes as opportunities to develop rather than indications of personal defeat. Holding onto guilt creates additional emotional burdens which slow your progress. Through self-forgiveness you achieve a weightless state that enables better wisdom and gentle movement toward your future.

People must choose either to live with constant self-harassment concerning their past mistakes or to validate their mistakes so they can move ahead with knowledge gained. The choice is yours. Throwing away guilt demands an initial struggle but leads to better things every time.

Guilty emotions dictate self-forgiveness to express love toward oneself. Giving yourself the respect and motivation that you would give to a dear friend represents self-forgiveness. Desist from casting judgment on your own shortcomings since your role should involve being your most devoted champion. Tell yourself that life permits human development alongside blunders and personal advancements.

Some of the errors we currently punish ourselves for will evolve into funny tales that we recall in future years. A crucial moment arrived when you mistakenly sent a message intended for your closest companion instead of your superior. You goofed in front of others while trying to recall their name – once or even a second time? The real-time humiliation turns into hysterical future reminiscence. By accepting your own mistakes with a sense of humor self-forgiveness will become less challenging to achieve.

Take deep breaths before remembering that mistakes will never create your identity. Your capacity to advance while learning and continuing forward matters more than anything else. Release feelings of guilt and absorb the important lessons before advancing with self-compassion. Life's great journey demands a combination of making progress and being resilient alongside having a humorous perspective rather than pursuing perfection.

Chapter 19

Self-Care Without the Guilt

> **Almost everything will work again if you unplug it for a few minutes, including you."**
>
> — *Anne Lamott*

In a world obsessed with productivity, self-care often feels like an indulgence. You decide to take a break, only to be haunted by that nagging voice in your head whispering, "Shouldn't you be doing something more *productive*?" The truth stands that pursuing personal care leads to productivity. The energy that drives your activity combined with the relief your body needs and mind crave, and spirit seeks resets your whole self. Its absence reduces you to the equivalent of a smartphone operating with just 1% power before it must close due to notifications.

Practicing self-care consists of necessary measures rather than being an unproductive habit. The goal is to find equilibrium between life's requirements while maintaining enough vitality and mental clarity. Let's dive into how to practice self-care without letting guilt tag along for the ride.

The Guilt Trap: Why We Feel Bad About Resting

For many of us, resting feels wrong because society glorifies the grind. We're bombarded with messages like, "Hustle harder!" or "Sleep is for the weak!" (Whoever said that has clearly never met a sleep-deprived human.)

Guilt sneaks in when we equate our worth with our output. We think if we're not ticking items off a to-do list, we're failing. But here's the thing: rest isn't the opposite of work—it's what makes work possible. Self-care isn't a luxury; it's a necessity.

Guilt-Free Self-Care Practices

Self-care doesn't have to be elaborate or expensive. It can be as simple as taking a deep breath or as luxurious as a spa day. The key is to focus on activities that truly nourish your body, mind, and soul.

1. **For the Body:**
   - ☐ Take a guilt-free nap. (More on this later!)
   - ☐ Enjoy a slow yoga session or a walk in nature without checking your step count.
   - ☐ Indulge in your favorite dessert—no calorie counting allowed!

2. **For the Mind:**
   - ☐ Spend 10 minutes reading something purely for fun.
   - ☐ Watch your favorite sitcom rerun without multitasking. (Yes, binge-watching *Friends* again is valid self-care.)

- ☐ Doodle, color, or try a puzzle to relax your brain.

3. **For the Soul:**
    - ☐ Meditate or simply sit in silence for a few minutes.
    - ☐ Connect with a loved one just to chat, not to solve problems.
    - ☐ Journal about things you're grateful for—big or small.

Example: The Guilt-Ridden Nap That Changed Everything

My close friend Priya is the prime example of someone who constantly achieves great things. Overachievers have an ideal representative in Priya who symbolizes this category perfectly. She constantly handles office work assignments together with social events and her continuous pursuit to feel productive. On that completely draining week Priya decided to take a brief rest by lying down. A thirty-minute rest change her mood to panic when she awoke.

She made her announcement with shock after her thirty-minute rest as if it were a massive misdeed. She began describing each activity that could have replaced her rest session. A miracle occurred when she experienced wonderful feelings. Her headache vanished and her mood brightened beside the decrease in the intimidating appearance of her to-do list. That guilt-ridden nap? The nap gave her entire day a positive transfrmation.

Priya's takeaway: sometimes the most productive thing you can do is rest.

How to Ditch the Guilt for Good

1. **Reframe Self-Care as Essential:**
    Think of self-care like charging your phone. Would you feel guilty about plugging it in? No, because you know it's necessary for it to work. The same goes for you.

2. **Set Boundaries:**
    Block off time for self-care in your schedule and treat it like an unmissable appointment.

3. **Celebrate Small Wins:**
    Even five minutes of self-care is a victory. Didn't have time for a spa day? A five-minute stretch counts.

4. **Give Yourself Permission:**
    Literally say, "I give myself permission to rest." It sounds silly, but it works.

5. **Laugh It Off:**
    When guilt creeps in, laugh at it. Remind yourself that the world won't collapse because you took a nap or spent an hour painting badly.

The Humor in Self-Care

Self-care isn't always Instagram-worthy, and that's okay. Sometimes it's lighting a candle and meditating; other times, it's eating ice cream in your pajamas while watching a trashy reality show.

Remember that time you thought a bubble bath would be the pinnacle of relaxation, only to drop your phone in the water while trying to take a picture? Or when you attempted yoga and got stuck in a pose, only to have your dog "help" by licking your face? That's self-care, too. It's messy, real, and worth it.

Final Thought: You Deserve to Recharge

Self-care without guilt is about recognizing that your value isn't measured by how much you accomplish in a day. You are not a machine that exists to check off tasks—you are a human being who needs moments of rest, joy, and stillness to function at your best.

When we deny ourselves rest, we run on empty, pushing through exhaustion and stress until burnout forces us to stop. But what if, instead of seeing self-care as an obstacle to productivity, we saw it as the foundation for it? What if, instead of feeling guilty for resting, we felt empowered by it?

Taking care of yourself doesn't mean neglecting your responsibilities—it means showing up for them with renewed energy, focus, and enthusiasm. It means understanding that a well-rested, happy, and fulfilled version of you is far more effective than a drained and overworked one.

So, the next time you feel that pang of guilt creeping in as you take a break, remind yourself: **you're not being lazy—you're refueling.** The world won't stop because you took a breath, but your ability to show up as your best self will improve because you did.

At the end of the day, life isn't just about getting things done—it's about enjoying the journey, being kind to yourself, and making space for the moments that bring you peace. Because when you care for yourself, you're not just benefiting you—you're bringing your best, most balanced self to everything and everyone around you.

Chapter 20
The Compassionate Inner Voice

> **Be careful how you are talking to yourself because you are listening."**
>
> – *Lisa M. Hayes*

Do you know that voice inside your head? The one that narrates your life, critiques your every move, and sometimes sounds like a snarky movie critic. For many of us, our inner voice is more like a drill sergeant than a cheerleader. But here's the truth: that inner voice has *immense* power. It can either lift you up or tear you down. And cultivating a compassionate, nurturing inner voice is one of the most transformative things you can do for yourself.

Let's be honest: we often speak to ourselves in ways we'd never dream of speaking to a friend. Would you tell your bestie, "Wow, way to go, genius—you can't even parallel park!" or "Of course, you failed that. What did you expect?" Probably not. Yet, we say these things to ourselves all the time.

But what if we flipped the script? What if we treated ourselves with the same kindness and encouragement, we offer others? That's the magic of the compassionate inner voice.

The Power of a Kind Inner Dialogue

The therapeutic voice does not function by disregarding faults or maintaining artificial perfection. The purpose of building this compassionate voice is turning tough times into chances for personal development. It's about saying, "It's okay. You're learning. You'll get through this."

A gentle inner voice helps you create the most powerful fan you have since you stop tearing yourself down. The shift improves your feeling without only improving but also increasing your resilience and self-esteem and producing greater happiness.

Techniques to Cultivate Your Inner Cheerleader

1. **Catch the Critic:**
   The first step is awareness. Notice when your inner voice takes a negative turn. For example, if you spill coffee on your shirt, instead of, "Ugh, I'm such a mess," pause and reframe it: "Well, looks like I'm starting the day with a little adventure!"

2. **Talk to Yourself Like a Friend:**
   Ask yourself: What would I say to a friend in this situation? If a friend was nervous about a presentation, you'd say, "You're going to rock this! You've got this!" Now, try saying that to yourself.

3. **Practice Positive Affirmations:**
   Create a list of affirmations that resonate with you, like "I am capable," "I am enough," or "I learn from every experience." Repeat them daily, even if they feel cheesy at first.

4. **Humor as a Shield:**
    When your inner critic shows up, disarm it with humor. If your mind says, "You're going to fail," respond with, "Thanks for the pep talk, but I think I'll pass on the doom and gloom today."

5. **Celebrate Small Wins:**
    When you accomplish something—even if it's just surviving Monday—acknowledge it. Say, "Look at me go!" or "I crushed that like a pro!" Small celebrations create a habit of positivity.

Example: The Power of a Pep Talk

Let me tell you about my friend Ravi. Ravi is a brilliant guy, but his inner voice has a flair for drama. One day, he was trying to assemble a bookshelf from a certain *famous Swedish furniture store*. As he stared at the cryptic instructions, his inner critic chimed in: "You're going to mess this up. Why did you even think you could do this?"

But instead of spiraling, Ravi decided to channel his inner cheerleader. He stood up, dramatically pointed to the pile of wooden planks, and said aloud, "Ravi, you *got this*! You're basically an engineer. Those IKEA pieces don't stand a chance!"

Did he get it right on the first try? Of course not. The shelf ended up backward, and he had to start over. But instead of berating himself, he laughed and said, "This is just part of my hero's journey!" With a little patience—and a lot of encouragement—Ravi eventually built the shelf. And yes, it's still standing.

Why Compassion Matters

Transforming your inner voice isn't just about feeling better—it's about living better. When you approach yourself with kindness, you're more likely to take risks, try new things, and bounce back from setbacks.

A nurturing inner voice gives you the confidence to say, "I'll try," instead of, "What's the point?" It reminds you that you're human, that mistakes are normal, and that progress is more important than perfection.

The Humor in Self-Talk

Your internal cheerleader sometimes reaches over top of comfort, but it remains suitable. Hyping yourself up for simple activities becomes possible when you say "You are a fabric-folding warrior" for doing the laundry. You successfully dominate your sock task right now. Sure, it's silly—but silly works.

We should accept those small yet awkward situations that occur during affirmations use. There are times when you must state your positive declarations aloud which leads others to hear them when you are in public settings. A forceful inner affirmation floats from your mouth as you shop in the grocery aisle before a random shopper responds by saying "Yes you are." The humorous nature of self-affirmations acts as a weight reliever throughout this experience.

Final Thought: Be Your Own Biggest Fan

The inner voice follows you throughout each challenge you face and during your successes and minor failures that happen between them. Hence instead of pointing fingers with doubts and criticisms your inner voice should function as positive reinforcement.

Existing life brings enough external obstacles so it should not host supplementary inner challenges. Other obstacles and rejections already exist in life so you should not fight your inner voice while it continuously pulls you downward. Changing the way, you speak to yourself will enable you to live a better life than you can possibly imagine. Through self-compassion your mind will grant you strength to pursue new opportunities and to recover from failure by becoming more resilient.

Through self-kindness you develop an internal shelter that enables mistakes to serve as lessons while you value all your shortcomings and need not achieve perfection for self-acceptance.

Always check whether the statements your critical voice conveys to yourself would apply when sharing them with a friend. If not, respond with kindness instead. Rephrase negative thoughts using kindness when the answer to your self-question is no. You must cheer for yourself during your mistakes while laughing at your errors before reminding yourself that progress requires multiple attempted efforts full of patience and love.

Whenever life ends you will spend your entire existence together with your true self. Establish a positive nurturing and supportive relationship because self-worth demands this kind of treatment.

Part 6

EMBRACING THE JOURNEY

Chapter 21
The Beauty of Imperfection

> **" Have no fear of perfection—
> you'll never reach it."**
>
> *– Salvador Dalí*

When was the last time you had a "perfect" day? You know, the kind where your alarm goes off on time, you nail your morning routine, and everything on your to-do list gets checked off without a hitch? Can't remember? Neither can I. That's because life doesn't happen in perfection—it happens in the glorious, messy, unpredictable moments in between.

The truth is, perfection is an illusion. Trying to achieve it is like chasing a rainbow: beautiful to imagine but impossible to catch. And honestly, would we even want perfection if we could have it? Imperfections are what make us human, what give life its charm, and what teach us to grow.

Let's shift the narrative: balance and growth aren't about flawlessly "arriving" at some mythical destination of perfection. They're about embracing the stumbles, the detours, and the laughs along the way.

Why Imperfection is Beautiful

Imperfections aren't flaws—they're features. Our distinctive characteristics along with our realness and enhanced fascinating quality distinguish us as distinct individuals. The world becomes monotonous when everything follows the original plan. It sounds nice for about five minutes, but then what? No surprises, no challenges, no funny stories to share at dinner parties.

The true spell of life develops from all our human imperfections. We develop our inner strength together with creativity as well as discover our humorous nature through the unexpected moments in our life. The mishaps from life serve as opportunities to gain self-forgiveness which paves our path toward future progress.

How to Embrace Imperfection

1. **Ditch the Myth of Perfect Balance:**
   Balance requires individuals to maintain different elements of their life in alignment while acknowledging moments of imbalance. Adjustment and adaptation serve as the basis for discovering solutions that function in the present moment. On certain days you might excel at your workout routines despite missing your meditation practice. Other days, it's a meditation win and cereal for dinner. That's life, and it's beautiful.

2. **Celebrate the Quirks:**
   Those little imperfections you see as "flaws" are often the very things that others find endearing about you. Embrace your quirks—whether it's

your inability to fold a fitted sheet or your talent for getting lost even with GPS.

3. **Reframe "Failure" as Learning:**
    When something doesn't go as planned, ask yourself, "What can I learn from this?" Mistakes are just stepping stones to growth. Remember, every great success story has a chapter that starts with, "And then everything went wrong..."

4. **Find Humor in the Chaos:**
    When life throws you curveballs, laugh. Missed the train? Spilled coffee on your shirt? Forgot your umbrella during a downpour? These moments might feel frustrating at the time, but they make for the best stories later.

Example: The Perfect Morning Routine Gone Wrong

Let me tell you about my friend Ananya. She decided to revamp her mornings after reading *every* self-help blog on morning routines. Her plan was flawless: wake up at 6 a.m., do yoga, journal, meditate, make a smoothie, and read a chapter of a book—all before 7 a.m.

Day one arrived. The alarm rang, but instead of gracefully rolling out of bed, she hit snooze... four times. She finally got up at 6:45, only to realize she couldn't find her yoga mat. She tried journaling, but her pen ran out of ink. The blender for her smoothie? Broken. By 7:30, Ananya was sitting on the floor, laughing at herself while eating a slightly questionable granola bar.

Here's the best part: she realized she didn't need the *perfect* routine to start her day. The laughter and self-compassion she found in the chaos were more energizing than any green smoothie ever could be.

The Continuous Journey

We often see life as a series of destinations: the perfect job, the perfect relationship, the perfect version of ourselves. But life isn't about arriving—it's about the journey. It's about growing, learning, and evolving, one imperfect step at a time.

Every setback is a lesson. Every detour is an adventure. And every flaws is an opportunity to connect more deeply with yourself and others.

The Humor in Imperfections

Let's face it: some of life's best moments come from things not going as planned. Like the time I tried to bake a cake for a friend's birthday and ended up with something that looked—and tasted—like a burnt frisbee. We laughed so hard that we forgot about the cake and just ate ice cream instead.

Imperfections are life's way of reminding us not to take things too seriously. They keep us humble, grounded, and real.

Final Thought: Perfectly Imperfect

The beauty of imperfection is that it makes life richer, more colorful, and infinitely more interesting. If everything went according to plan all the time, we'd never experience the unexpected joys, the hilarious mishaps, or the moments of growth that shape who we are. Imperfections don't make us less—they make us more.

Think about your favorite memories. Do you recall your them from moments of flawless events or from points when unexpected events occurred? Your hidden discovery of a stunning location emerged during that time you accidentally lost yourself on the journey. During your presentation when you messed up your speech delivery you somehow managed to create amused and entertained reactions from your audience. Memorable moments never stem from flawless situations because genuine real-life experiences mark these memories.

You should breathe deeply and decide to release perfectionist dreams the instant you find yourself pursuing unattainable excellence. Achieve self-authorization as a continuous project of self-improvement. Accept the untidy aspects of existence alongside your special features and all the challenging events that cause personal transformation.

When things don't go as planned, instead of feeling frustrated, try to smile and say, "This is just part of my beautifully imperfect journey." Because that's exactly what life is—a journey, not a perfectly curated highlight reel.

The magic happens through imperfections according to Ananya's morning routine which can serve as a constant reminder to us all. Your best moments sometimes arrive when smoothies stay unprepared, and journal pages stay blank while you encounter amusing moments by enjoying granola bars as you remain in the right spot in life.

Chapter 22
Celebrating Small Wins

 Success is a series of small wins."

– John C. Maxwell

Life is full of grand achievements—graduations, promotions, weddings—but let's be real: those big moments are few and far between. What really keeps us going are the little victories, the everyday triumphs that might not earn us a standing ovation but absolutely deserve a happy dance in the kitchen.

Celebrating small wins is more than just a feel-good moment; it's a powerful way to build momentum, boost confidence, and find joy in the process of growth. It's about recognizing that every step forward, no matter how tiny, is still progress.

Why Small Wins Matter

Small wins are like breadcrumbs on the path of life. They might not seem important on their own, but together, they create a path that leads to significant changes. Think of them as the unsung heroes of your journey—the little victories that remind you you're moving in the right direction, even when the major achievements remain distant.

Celebrating these wins is also a mindset shift. It trains you to focus on what's going right instead of fixating on what's not. Over time, this positive reinforcement builds resilience, motivation, and—most importantly—a sense of gratitude for the journey itself.

How to Celebrate Small Wins

1. **Recognize the Victory:**
    The first step is simply noticing when you've achieved something, no matter how minor it seems. Finished a task you've been procrastinating on? That's a win. Got through a stressful day without losing your cool? Win. Managed to water the plants before they turned into crispy relics? Major win.

2. **Acknowledge Your Effort:**
    It's not just about the result—it's about the effort you put in to get there. Celebrate the fact that you tried, even if the outcome wasn't perfect.

3. **Make It Fun:**
    Your celebrations don't have to be elaborate. Do a little dance, treat yourself to your favorite snack, or blast your favorite song. The point is to associate the win with a burst of joy.

4. **Keep Track:**
    Write down your small wins in a journal or a note on your phone. On tough days, revisiting that list can remind you of how far you've come.

Example: The Great Cooking Triumph

Let me tell you about my friend Rohan, a self-proclaimed disaster in the kitchen. After countless failed attempts at cooking (think charred eggs and "soup" that was more like flavored water), he finally decided to tackle a simple recipe: pasta with marinara sauce.

It seemed foolproof, but halfway through, he realized he'd forgotten to buy marinara sauce. Undeterred, he Googled a recipe and tried to make his own. The result? A kitchen covered in tomato splatters, a sauce that was suspiciously orange, and a slightly overcooked pile of pasta.

But here's the thing: it was edible. And for Rohan, that was a win. He celebrated by snapping a picture of his creation, sending it to all his friends, and declaring himself "Chef Extraordinaire." It didn't matter that the sauce was more like chunky juice—what mattered was that he'd tried, and he'd succeeded.

Why Celebrating Small Wins is a Game-Changer

1. **They Build Confidence:**
    Each small win reminds you that you're capable, which motivates you to keep going.

2. **They Create Momentum:**
    Success breeds success. Celebrating small wins gives you the energy to tackle bigger challenges.

3. **They Make the Journey Enjoyable:**
    Life isn't just about reaching the finish line—it's about enjoying the race. Small wins are like

the water stations along the way, keeping you hydrated and happy.

The Humor in Small Wins

Let's not forget the sheer comedy that often accompanies these moments. Like the time I successfully folded a fitted sheet after 27 attempts, only to realize I'd folded it inside out. Or the day I managed to assemble an IKEA chair without any leftover screws—only to sit on it and hear an ominous creak.

These little victories might not seem significant to anyone else, but to me, they were monumental. And the best part? They gave me a reason to laugh and celebrate, imperfections and all.

Final Thought: The Power of Tiny Triumphs

Big achievements may make the headlines of our lives, but it's the small wins that fill the pages. They're the quiet victories that remind us we're making progress, even when it doesn't feel like it. Celebrating small wins isn't just about feeling good in the moment—it's about creating a mindset that sees every step forward, no matter how small, as valuable.

Think about it: if you wait to celebrate only the *big* moments, you'll spend most of your life in a state of waiting. But when you acknowledge and appreciate the little things—the email you finally sent, the workout you didn't skip, the fact that you made it through a tough day— you turn everyday life into a series of tiny triumphs.

Progress isn't always dramatic. Sometimes, it's just choosing to keep going. And that, in itself, is worth celebrating. So the next time you do something—anything—that moves you even an inch forward, take a moment to recognize it. Maybe even do a little happy dance. Because life isn't just about the finish line—it's about every step along the way.

Chapter 23
The Infinite Nature of Balance

> 66 Happiness is not a matter of intensity but of balance, order, rhythm, and harmony."
>
> *– Thomas Merton*

Balance—it's that elusive goal we're all striving for, whether we're trying to juggle work and family, healthy eating and indulgent desserts, or meditation and Netflix binges. But here's the truth: balance isn't a one-time achievement. It's not like crossing a finish line where you can proudly declare, "I am officially balanced!" and call it a day.

Instead, balance is a lifelong dance. Sometimes it's graceful, and sometimes it's more of a chaotic flail, but that's the beauty of it. It's a dynamic process, a constant ebb and flow where the goal isn't perfection but progress.

Why Balance is a Lifelong Practice

The truth is that existence remains unpredictable. Everything works smooth until one sudden moment when your to-do list expands uncontrollably while your dog devours your headphones then you discover you have two appointments at the same time.

The ability to handle unpredictable situations describes what balance really is. One must acknowledge that life's equilibrium shifted naturally is perfectly acceptable. Your ability to adapt and move your focus to key areas stands as the essential factor more than getting everything right at first. You need to accept that finding balance means repeating this process continuously.

Challenges: The Art of Constant Adjustments

Challenges aren't roadblocks—they're recalibration points. They remind us to pause, reassess, and adjust. Whether it's a demanding work deadline, a relationship hiccup, or simply forgetting to eat lunch, each challenge is an opportunity to rediscover what balance looks like in that moment.

Think of balance as riding a bicycle. You don't achieve perfect stillness and coast along forever. Instead, you're constantly making tiny adjustments to keep moving forward. Some days, you might feel like a Tour de France champion, and other days, you might wobble into a bush. Both are part of the journey.

Example: The Quest for the "Perfect" Balance

Take my friend Priya, for example. She decided she was going to master balance in her life. She planned out her "perfect week" with military precision:

- Wake up at 5 a.m. every day for yoga.
- Meal-prep superfoods for breakfast, lunch, and dinner.
- Work with laser focus for 8 hours straight.

- Meditate for 30 minutes before bed.

For two whole days, Priya nailed it. She felt like a glowing, Zen goddess. But by day three, life happened. She overslept, skipped yoga, ate a bag of chips for lunch, and fell asleep halfway through her meditation.

At first, she felt like a failure. But then it hit her—balance wasn't about sticking rigidly to her plan. It was about rolling with the punches and making space for flexibility. So, instead of beating herself up, Priya laughed it off, ordered pizza for dinner, and decided to tackle yoga the next day.

The Beauty of the Process

Balance exists only because its duration never stays static. Maintaining balance never ends since it requires everyday work. Every modification and adaptation creates resilience while letting you understand yourself better and enables you to discover moments of happiness throughout your journey.

Working on balance helps you understand the value of reaching minor goals. You accomplished sustaining your emotional equilibrium even though you missed some objectives throughout the day. That, too, is balance.

The Humor in Seeking Balance

Let's not ignore the hilarity that often accompanies the pursuit of balance. Like the time I tried to follow a morning routine that included journaling, yoga, and making a green smoothie, only to realize I'd forgotten to actually drink the smoothie before rushing out the door. Or the day I set aside 30 minutes for "self-care" and spent it scrolling through memes about self-care.

These moments are a reminder that balance isn't about being flawless—it's about finding the humor in the chaos and moving forward anyway.

Final Thought: The Infinite Journey

Balance is not something we achieve once and for all—it's an ongoing process, a rhythm we learn to dance to rather than a fixed state we reach. Life is constantly shifting, throwing new responsibilities, challenges, and surprises our way, and true balance lies in our ability to adapt, reset, and keep moving forward.

A balanced day resembles a well-designed organizational system which leads to execution success. On certain days the only objective becomes surviving while maintaining a humorous and graceful attitude. The goal of balance comes from finding enough room for important matters as they present themselves in different moments.

People who practice balance throughout their lives do not place themselves in rigid goals because this mindset lets them change and explore new possibilities. We develop better acceptance toward unplanned days while we start celebrating all meaningful achievements regardless of their size. The daily renewal of life enables us to recognize present living above perfection because every new day provides us with another chance to rediscover our equilibrium.

Your level of equilibrium today determines nothing about your balance as getting everything right isn't the standard. The important thing is to attend each day and modify our approach while appreciating what we learn during the journey. Balancing requires learning how to navigate life's movements since reaching complete stillness does not define beauty.

Chapter 24
Embracing the Unknown

> **A ship in harbor is safe, but that is not what ships are built for."**
>
> – *John A. Shedd*

Life is like a giant mystery novel—unpredictable, exciting, and sometimes downright confusing. The unknown can be intimidating. It's that moment when you stand at the edge of your comfort zone, peering into the great abyss of "What if?" But here's the thing: the unknown isn't your enemy. It's your greatest teacher.

When you embrace uncertainty with curiosity and openness, you invite growth, creativity, and adventure into your life. It's not about knowing all the answers—it's about being brave enough to explore the questions.

The Beauty of Uncertainty

Uncertainty gets a bad rap. We often see it as a threat, something to fear or avoid. But what if we flipped the script? What if we viewed the unknown as an invitation to grow, evolve, and discover parts of ourselves we never knew existed?

Think about it: every meaningful experience in life started with a step into the unknown. Your first job, your first relationship, or even trying that weird-looking dish at a restaurant—all were leaps of faith into uncharted territory.

And more often than not, those leaps lead to something rewarding (even if the dish didn't).

The beauty of uncertainty lies in its potential. It's the space where dreams take shape, where possibilities are endless, and where you get to learn what you're truly capable of.

The Courage to Leap

Stepping into the unknown takes courage. It's like jumping into a pool without being entirely sure if the water is warm. But here's the secret: even if the water is chilly at first, you'll adapt. You'll find your rhythm, and you might even discover that you're a stronger swimmer than you thought.

Growth doesn't happen in the comfort zone. It happens when you take that leap of faith—when you say yes to an opportunity, even if you don't have all the details figured out.

Example: Taking the Leap

Take my friend Raj, for instance. Raj had spent ten years in a steady corporate job, climbing the ladder and checking all the "success" boxes. But deep down, he felt restless. He'd always dreamed of starting his own business, but the thought of leaving his stable paycheck for the unknown terrified him.

One day, after much internal debate (and an inspiring conversation with his dog), Raj took the plunge. He quit his job and launched a small graphic design studio from his living room. The first few months were rocky—he had to juggle late nights, tight budgets, and the occasional "What have I done?!" moment.

But as time passed, things started to click. Raj's creativity flourished, clients began rolling in, and he found himself more fulfilled than ever. The leap into the unknown didn't just change his career; it transformed his life.

How to Embrace the Unknown

If the idea of stepping into uncertainty makes you break out in a nervous sweat, don't worry—you're not alone. Here are some tips to make the unknown feel a little less daunting:

1. **Start Small**
    You don't have to move to a new country or change careers overnight. Start with something manageable, like trying a new hobby or striking up a conversation with a stranger.

2. **Reframe Fear as Excitement**
    The butterflies in your stomach? They're not fear—they're anticipation. Channel that energy into curiosity and see where it takes you.

3. **Focus on Growth, Not Perfection**
    It's not about nailing it on the first try. It's about learning, adapting, and growing along the way.

4. **Find Your Cheerleaders**
    Surround yourself with people who believe in you and encourage you to take risks. Sometimes, a little nudge from a friend can make all the difference.

The Humor in the Unknown

Of course, stepping into the unknown isn't always glamorous. Sometimes, it's hilariously awkward. Like the time I signed up for a salsa class to "embrace the unknown" and spent the first session stepping on my partner's toes so many times that they started calling me "Twinkle Toes."

But here's the thing: those moments of imperfection are what make the journey memorable. They remind us that it's okay to stumble as long as we keep moving forward.

Final Thought: The Gift of the Unknown

The unknown renders itself not as a domain of dread but instead establishes itself as the region where practically limitless possibilities rest. Through dreams we launch, and growth emerges and unforgettable life moments' walk through this threshold.

People seek assurance by believing knowledge about future events will provide them serenity. Self-fulfillment stems from embracing opportunities and conducting self-discovery through practical experience so we can demonstrate our exceeding our initial expectations. The unknown provides beauty because it pushes humans to advance through life. When we face uncertainty, we develop new abilities as we exceed our known boundaries to create narratives we could not have envisioned before.

All unpredicted transitions into the unknown domain will they progress with ease? Of course not. Several unknown endeavors will be disheveled while others will produce comical outcomes and others will transport us to unpredictable destinations. The enchantment lies within the fact that every path we choose along with each mistake we encounter, and surprising diversion creates a journey that belongs to only us.

Before taking another leap into the unknown make sure to breathe deeply then embolden yourself with courage. The unknown existence should be seen as something that brings opportunities rather than fear. And who knows? Your existence can transform into its most rewarding period through this step.

Chapter 25
A Call to Begin

> **The journey of a thousand miles begins with a single step."**
>
> *– Lao Tzu*

You've made it this far, and now we're at the final chapter. But don't think for a second that this is the end. Oh no, this is the beginning. In fact, the real story starts now. Everything we've discussed—the growth, the balance, the gratitude—is like a road map. But it's up to you to start walking the path. And let me tell you, it's not going to be perfect. It might not even be pretty. But I promise you, it's going to be worth it.

You're about to take that first step. The small one. The seemingly insignificant action that will set everything else into motion. Maybe it's stretching in the morning, journaling about your day, or even just deciding to breathe deeply and be present for a moment. Whatever it is, it's your step. And that's where everything changes.

The Power of the First Step

You see, the first step is a big deal. Not because it's complicated or earth-shattering, but because it's a commitment to start the journey. The first step is where courage meets curiosity, where intentions become actions.

And while it might seem simple, it's the one thing that gets the ball rolling.

Take my cousin Priya, for example. Priya always wanted to get fit but couldn't seem to find the time. For years, she kept saying, "Tomorrow I'll start." Sound familiar? Well, one day, she decided that tomorrow wasn't coming anytime soon. So she took a tiny step—she put on her sneakers and walked around the block. That was it. No marathon, no gym membership. Just a walk.

Now, Priya walks every day. And not just around the block—she's up to 5 kilometers a day, and she even runs some of it. Who knew that one small step would lead to a whole new lifestyle? But that's how it works. Start small, and suddenly, you're living big.

The Fear of Taking the First Step

I get it. The first step can feel daunting. It's like looking at a mountain and thinking, "I could never climb that." But here's the thing: you don't need to climb the mountain all at once. You just need to take one step. And then another. And another.

Remember when I told you about my stretch routine? That first morning, I thought, "What if I can't even touch my toes?" But you know what happened? I stretched. I didn't touch my toes—let's not get ahead of ourselves—but I felt better. A little bit lighter. A little more energized. And the next day, I stretched again. And the next.

If you wait until you're ready, you'll be waiting forever. But if you take that first step, you'll be amazed at how quickly you adapt. And before you know it, you're no longer just imagining the change—you're living it.

How to Take That First Step

Okay, so how do you actually take that first step? Here are a few tips that might help you get going:

1. **Make It Ridiculously Easy**
    Want to start journaling? Don't commit to an hour a day. Start with five minutes. Want to be more grateful? Write down one thing you're thankful for. It's easy, it's quick, and it's effective.

2. **Give Yourself Permission to Be Imperfect**
    You don't have to get it right on the first try. In fact, you probably won't. But that's part of the fun. It's like trying to cook a new recipe. Your first attempt might look like something from a horror movie, but the next one will be better.

3. **Find Your Cheerleaders**
    Everyone needs a support squad. Find someone who'll encourage you when you feel like giving up. Sometimes, a "You got this!" from a friend is all it takes to make that first step feel a little less scary.

4. **Celebrate Small Wins**
    Don't wait until you've achieved the grand goal. Celebrate the little victories—like getting out of bed on time or writing your first sentence in a journal. Each step counts.

The Humor in the First Step

Let's be honest taking the first step can be hilarious. It's usually a bit awkward, a little clumsy, and maybe even slightly embarrassing. Like the time I tried meditating for the first time and ended up falling asleep in the middle of my session. I woke up, startled, thinking I had missed an hour, only to find out it had been five minutes.

But here's the thing: those awkward, imperfect moments are the ones we remember. They're the moments that remind us we're human. So don't be afraid to laugh at yourself. In fact, laugh at yourself as much as possible—it makes the whole journey a lot more fun.

Final Thought: The Adventure Awaits

So, here's your challenge: take that first step. It doesn't matter how small or seemingly insignificant it may be— what matters is that you take it. Maybe it's stretching for five minutes, writing down a single thought in your journal, or simply deciding to be more present in your daily life. Whatever it is, it's yours to define. And in doing so, you set something powerful in motion.

Because here's the truth: life isn't shaped by grand, sweeping changes. It's built on the tiny, consistent steps we take every day. The moments where we choose progress over perfection. The times we decide to show up for ourselves, even when it's messy, uncertain, or downright awkward.

Looking back, you'll realize that those little actions— the ones that felt almost too small to matter—were the ones that led you to something extraordinary. You don't need to have everything figured out. You don't need to see the whole path. You just need to begin.

So go ahead, take that first step. Step into the unknown. Step toward growth. Step into the adventure that is your life. Who knows where it will lead?

And just like that, the greatest journey of all begins—one step at a time.

Epilogue:
Your Journey Begins Now

And just like that, we're at the last page. But if there's one thing, I want you to remember, it's this: the real journey begins now. Not tomorrow. Not "one day." **Now.**

Development does not require flawless performance while existence never depends on waiting for the perfect opportunity. Your journey towards yourself starts by showing up at your current location while beginning anywhere you find yourself and taking that first step—however small it may be.

There will never be a grand sign from the universe saying, *"Now is the time, my child."* The only moment you truly have is now. The only person who can make the choice to begin—is you.

You've read the ideas, reflected on the insights, and maybe even laughed at the awkwardness of starting something new. Now, it's time to turn those thoughts into action. Because knowledge without action is like a gym membership you never use—full of potential, but ultimately useless if you don't show up.

The **Mahabharata** reminds us that transformation comes from effort, resilience, and the willingness to act. As Krishna tells Arjuna:

**"Uddhared ātmanātmānaṁ,
na ātmānam avasādayet"**
*("Lift yourself by yourself;
do not let yourself fall." – Bhagavad Gita 6.5)*

No one else can walk this path for you. No book, no mentor, no external force can create change unless you decide to take that first step. You are your own guide, your own strength, and your own greatest ally.

And since almost every chapter in this book had a touch of humor, how could I possibly miss out on the grand finale? So here's your final takeaway: self-improvement is like learning to dance. At first, you'll step on your own feet (and probably others' too). You'll feel awkward, unsure, maybe even a little ridiculous. But if you keep moving, step by step, one day you'll realize—you're actually dancing.

So, take that first step. Trip over your own feet if you must. But move. Because the adventure of becoming your best self-starts the moment you decide to begin.

Now go, lift yourself up, take action—and don't forget to laugh along the way.